Before you leave your church, before you spread rumors about your church, and before you abandon the church altogether, read *Called to Stay*. And before you blindly stay in the same religious rut you've been in your whole life, read *Called to Stay*. Caleb's call for us to love our churches—and God's Church as a whole—is important, passionate, and needed. If you read this book with an open mind, it just might change your perspective of what it means to be a church member.

Kyle Idleman, author of *Not a Fan* and *Gods at War*

This yellow book showcases a life-changing and God-glorifying adventure waiting for you in your own backyard. If you answer the call, you will be richly rewarded. We're excited for how *Called to Stay* will impact our generation.

Alex and Brett Harris, authors of *Do Hard Things* and founders of TheRebelution.com

Many of you have been abused, and so many are crying out for help. I hope you will refuse to be a victim and, instead, take up Caleb's challenge to be that help to others in the body of Christ.

Josh McDowell, author of *The Unshakable Truth* and *New Evidence That Demands a Verdict*

It's a rare book that is biblical, strategic, timely, well-written, and persuasive all at the same time. *Called to Stay* is such a book. We all wish our churches were better, but many Christians have become hypercritical and intolerant of the body of Christ. It's always easier to point out the problems and walk away rather than stay and humbly serve as part of the solution. I'm delighted Caleb Breakey has written this book, and I highly recommend it to young and old alike.

Randy Alcorn, author of *Heaven* and *Safely Home*

Caleb Breakey writes with wit and wisdom on the sensitive and important topic of why so many young adults leave the church. This is not only relevant to the next generation, but to some boomers too. *Called to Stay* is not preachy, but it is biblical. It's loaded with practical truth about how to follow Jesus.

Dan Reiland, author of *Amplified Leadership*

Caleb Breakey challenges readers to think about our role in the church and how to respond to the changing landscape of culture within the church today.

Margaret Feinberg, author of *Wonderstruck*

You can't love Jesus and hate his bride. The chu⌐ ⌐⌐⌐ ⌐⌐Christ, worthy of our commitment, and God's tool for His work young men like Caleb Breakey remind us of th

Called *to* STAY

Caleb Breakey

HARVEST HOUSE PUBLISHERS
EUGENE, OREGON

Cover by Harvest House Publishers Inc., Eugene, Oregon

Backcover author photo by Carole Farmen

Published in association with literary agent David Van Diest of D.C. Jacobson & Associates LLC, an Author Management Company.

CALLED TO STAY

Copyright © 2013 by Caleb Jennings Breakey
Published by Harvest House Publishers
Eugene, Oregon 97402
www.harvesthousepublishers.com

Library of Congress Cataloging-in-Publication Data
    Breakey, Caleb Jennings, 1986-
    Called to stay / Caleb Jennings Breakey.
        pages cm
    ISBN 978-0-7369-5542-3 (pbk.)
    ISBN 978-0-7369-5543-0 (eBook)
    1. Generation Y—Religious life. 2. Young adults—Religious life. 3. Church. 4. Christian life.
    I. Title.
    BV4529.2.B74 2013
    248.8'4—dc23
                                                                    2013002886

Printed in the United States of America

13 14 15 16 17 18 19 20 21 / VP-JH / 10 9 8 7 6 5 4 3 2 1

To Brittney, who infiltrates my life with love,
strength, and a faith that moves mountains.
I love you so much, sweetheart.

ACKNOWLEDGMENTS

To Brittney, who didn't just tolerate the long working days—but encouraged them.

To David, who didn't let what *was* stop him from believing in what *could be*.

To Sarah, who encapsulated the message of this book.

To Kathleen, who went out of her way to unearth an important message.

To the amazing folks at Harvest House Publishers, who dream big for Jesus.

To Pastor Steve, who spent countless hours he didn't have discipling a kid at DQ.

To my family at Spring Creek, who may never know how much I love them.

CONTENTS

I absolutely love trees. I feel like I have to, since I live right outside of Seattle and they are everywhere. If you live in western Washington, the two things you know best are coffee and trees. You can't turn left or right without seeing one of the two.

One thing you never see, though, is a tree by itself. Imagine for a second how weird that might look: huge landscape, but only one tree. If a storm came—with its wind, rain, and power—what do you think would happen to that tree? It'd get totally uprooted and break apart. But when the winds get heavy in Washington, do you know what I see? I see thousands of trees taking the brunt of that wind and spreading it amongst themselves. They bend a little together, but then come up strong together.

That's how I think the Church should be. We were created out of community (the Trinity) and for community. We weren't meant to walk alone. Because when we do, storms come and destroy. But when we're in the community of the Church, we bear one another's burdens and come up strong.

When I look at my life, I see times when I've been frustrated, hurt, and even a little damaged by the local church. But I also see dozens, if not hundreds, of times when the tangible power and presence of God has radiated beautifully through and in its community. This doesn't happen by accident.

In this beautiful book, Caleb Breakey gets real about all the reasons why we should love the Church—and what that actually implies about how we do life in the body of Christ. I'm thankful for him, his life, and his words. I pray they encourage you and gently stir in your heart a deep love to *stay*.

Jefferson Bethke, author of *Jesus>Religion*
and creator of *Why I Hate Religion, But Love Jesus*

Note: A portion of each purchase of *Called to Stay* will be donated to two ministries with which Jefferson is intimately involved: *For the King*, which helps college students see that we are made to live for Jesus, and *Claro*, which brings light to social injustice by making candles that raise funds for Kingdom causes.

PART 1

Why You Shouldn't Abandon the Body

CHAPTER 1

Save the Girl

A Good Thing Waiting to Happen

With three cops aiming two pistols and a shotgun at my bride, her hands shaking uncontrollably, I came to the conclusion that getting falsely accused for robbing a bank on your honeymoon is about as fun as dropping your phone in the toilet.

> If you are in Christ, you are in some intrinsic way wedded to the welfare of others...There is a sense where I am not perfected until you are perfected. We are not perfected until every child of the living God is perfected.
>
> David Powlison

But ever since those seven squad cars surrounded me and my wife, we've seen that story turned into a lead article in *Chicken Soup for the Soul*, an invitation to meet with the FBI, and a wild and crazy memory that we may never top until death do us part. The whole experience taught us something very important:

Even the worst things are good things waiting to happen.

So it is with the body of Christ.

It's been said that church is like a sausage factory—you're better off enjoying the bratwurst than actually touring the plant. And we all know why. Church can be revolting. There's no community, no authenticity. Too much judgment, too little grace. Action takes a backseat to appearance. The whole scene just leaves a bad taste. Jesus himself would burst through the doors and turn over tables.

Or would he?

If you believe your church is maliciously shaming God for personal gain, that's one thing. Turn the tables and leave.

But what if your church desperately needs love and truth because it doesn't know what it's doing? What if others in your church feel the same way you do but are too afraid to speak up? What if your church is a good thing waiting to happen?

This is what this book is about.

Lead Passionless Believers to Heart Change

Even as I write this, a thousand voices from my peers whisper and shout:

- I've tried being a "change agent" in my church. It doesn't work.

- Organized religion is dead—why even bother?

- If you only knew how hurt I am, you'd understand that staying in church is impossible.

- Church people burn you at the stake when you stop conforming to their hypocritical and judgmental ways.

- This is all fine for you, but God called me out of the church for a reason—and I'm not going back.

- I've messed up too many times for God to use me in my church.

- I've been stomped, belittled, and discriminated against by church hierarchies in ways you cannot even fathom.

I'm not here to argue against these deeply felt pains, nor am I here to rush you into something you're not ready for. I'm simply here to talk about an action-oriented lifestyle that mirrors Jesus, leads passionless believers to heart change, and draws out believers too timid to go all-in for Christ.

Yes, there are churches we should avoid: ones that twist the truth for personal gain, or blaspheme the Holy Spirit, or preach a gospel blatantly contrary to the Bible. But these churches are few and far between.

I'd even venture to say that for every church in which Jesus would turn tables, there are one hundred more in which he would enter and say: "He who has ears to hear, let him hear" (Matthew 11:15).

I know that's hard to swallow if you've been severely hurt by your church. Staying in your local church can be hard. Harder than quitting church, harder than forming your own church, perhaps even harder than sharing Jesus to a world that hates him. It might be the hardest thing you ever do.

> Some of the most gifted and potentially powerful Christians I know are right now at a Starbucks or at a bar somewhere griping about the church, too tainted by grief and bitterness to be of any use to anyone.[2]
>
> Stephen Mansfield

The church is the kid who will poke your eye as you're examining her wounds. Stomp your foot as you're bringing her medicine. Call you a baby as she sucks on her thumb.

But take heart: If undefiled religion is caring for those who cannot possibly repay you, how much more undefiled is religion that cares for stagnant brothers and sisters who can also be cruelly stubborn?

Deciding to live like Jesus in your church is like signing on for the Navy SEALs. You're going to want to quit. But if you make it through, honor and a deep sense of purpose await.

It isn't easy, but it's worth it.

Who Should Read This Book

The last thing I want to do is waste your time. Life is too short and eternity too long to waste an afternoon on a book that might not benefit you one hundred times more than you invest in it.

> We must not give in to the idea that the church will die. That idea is simply not biblical.[3]
>
> Ed Stetzer

So before we go further, I want to pinpoint two types of people who *must* read this book. If one of the paragraphs describes you, then I feel comfortable saying that this book has tremendous value for you.

The *Frustrated*: You go to church but are extremely frustrated. The pastor and congregation don't seem to emphasize living a life of full-throttle devotion to Jesus. The church may appear to love God, but when it comes to loving the lost, making disciples, teaching others to follow Jesus, and just *longing* for God, the body is severely lacking. You care for the people in your church but feel as though they're stuck in mediocrity. Church is a part of their lives, but Jesus is merely a part of their theology. You feel awkward bringing this up in conversation. You're filled with a sense of helplessness. Church no longer feels like a place of worship. You feel you might be better off in another church or perhaps no church at all.

The *Sieged*: You've left the church. You feel free and strong in your relationship with Christ, but have come under the fire of a Christian siege. Your family and friends worry about you and question your salvation, making it harder than ever to return. They don't understand your desire to follow Jesus and fully commit yourself to him. You're more accepted among the non-religious crowd than the religious crowd—just like Jesus. You wonder whether or not church has lost its relevance.

> Extraordinary people for God are simply ordinary people who are willing to be used.[4]
>
> Ed Stetzer

If you're the Frustrated or the Sieged, then you are the person we need at the front lines. Because I know you. I *am* you. I know your passion for Jesus. I know your desire to glorify him with your life. You have the potential to, through the power of Christ, affect more lives for the Savior than you ever thought possible.

That said, it takes an all-out, cross-carrying, fully committed follower of Jesus to ignite this change.

And few of these followers remain in the body of Christ.

So here's my question. Is Jesus stirring you to infiltrate his church with passionate commitment?

Introduction to Infiltration

Whether you've left the church in a quest for more God, quietly attended every week but are uninvolved and disgruntled, or are wholly committed but simply frustrated, you're not alone.

Hundreds of people will probably abandon the church by the time you're finished reading this book. They're tired and hurting and only see one direction: the exit. What they fail to see is that leaving a sick person is easy.

Healing her is hard.

But just staying in church doesn't do anyone any good. It's what we do in our churches—intentionally, like Jesus—that matters. Problem is, few of us are doing it. In fact, we're running from it.

This book is a manifesto to stop running and start doing what Jesus has commanded of us. It's a compass for not only loving the church as Christ loved her, but also for bringing back stagnant believers who've wandered away from their first love—Jesus Christ.

I call this infiltration.

Because, similar to planting and watering seed, stirring a greater commitment to Jesus in your spiritual peers is done surreptitiously and gradually as you wait on God to orchestrate growth.

You don't have to be a super Christian to infiltrate. All you need is *desire*...

- to love God with all of your heart, soul, strength, and mind...even if you're still figuring out what that looks like in life.
- to love other people...even if it feels impossible.

If you've got these desires, then you've got my heart. I've been praying for you. Because you've got what it takes to do something that's so much more than just another movement. You've got what it takes to shift the Christian culture back to Jesus in a way that's real and sustainable. You are a follower, and it's time for you to start radiating the presence of Christ not only to the lost people of this world, but also to every last brother and sister in the body.

Every member serves the whole body, either to its health or to its destruction. This is no mere theory; it is a spiritual reality.[5]

Dietrich Bonhoeffer

This book isn't about stopping you from leaving the church. It's about helping you follow Jesus.

It just so happens that the more you follow Jesus, the more likely you'll stay in church.

The Cure for Sedated Christianity

> And Jesus said, "Father, forgive them, for they know not what they do." And they cast lots to divide his garments (Luke 23:34).

A gigantic number of churchgoers today are sedated. We go to church without desperately longing for God's presence. We talk after church without getting into any deep spiritual or personal conversations. We do a church thing in the middle of the week because that's what you're supposed to do. Then we do it all over again.

This is sedated Christianity, and we're all guilty of it to an extent.

The strongest argument I know for why you and I should love and care about the Church is that Jesus does. The greatest motivation we could ever find for being passionately committed to the Church is that Jesus is passionately committed to the Church.[6]

Joshua Harris

Many feel that leaving the church is the cure to this problem. But the real cure is doing things that Jesus would do and saying things he would say.

Believers going through the motions are primed for life-change. I know because I used to be the deadest of them all—until someone said things and did things in front of me that rattled my soul with the true, pure, beautiful call of Jesus.

I was infiltrated, and my life has never been the same.

In the pages to follow you're going to explore how to be like Jesus in the church. This book isn't just about infiltrating sedated church culture or living so that the world can tell you are a follower of Christ. It's about thrusting yourself into the grand campaign God has for building his church. It's about following the way of Jesus, who didn't make his life about rebelling or acting like he had it together—but about washing feet and fearlessly speaking the truth in love.

And it's about rescuing believers just like me.

An Incredible Journey on a Road Less Traveled

I'm Caleb and my purpose is to live for Jesus—even though I mess up pretty good sometimes. If you were to peel back the skin of my soul, you'd find that...

> A person who is changed becomes an agent of change. They continue to grow, learn, and serve because they themselves have been changed.[7]
>
> Ed Stetzer

- Though I never shy away from the complexities of Scripture, I'm more interested in living out the great commandments and the great commission.

- Though I value tradition, I'm more interested in a heart of conviction.

- Though I love plans and strategies, I'm more interested in the supernatural promptings of God's Holy Spirit.

- Though I understand the differing opinions of denominations, I'm more interested in uniting the body of Christ.

For most of my life, I was everything that infuriates me in the church today: Loveless. Passionless. Full of head knowledge. Going through the motions. A lukewarm Christian thinking he was tight with God.

I never questioned what was preached, never questioned what was not preached, and never entertained the thought that another church might be more biblically accurate than mine.

But, little by little, through other believers who loved me through my filth, Christ chiseled away at my cold, indifferent heart. I started gushing about Jesus more. Praying more. Loving God and others more. Thirsting for the Word. Smiling.

I actually *felt* Christian, as though Jesus had really died for me, and had really left instructions for me. I felt that my life really had incredible purpose. So I made a decision: If Jesus was real, then I wanted to unashamedly live my life as though I'd meet him one day.

This is what I saw in my brothers and sisters who helped break me free of my sedation, and I desperately wanted it.

Infiltration complete.

From that time forward, God placed a burning desire in me to build his church… through *my* church. To be like Jesus not only Monday through Saturday, but also on Sundays. To be like Jesus not just to "the least of these," but to anyone who might be spiritually sedated. It's an incredible journey that too few choose to take.

My hope is that this book helps more followers of Jesus choose it.

> [Followers of Jesus] will give an account for whether or not we have gathered together regularly with the church, spurred the church on to love and good deeds, and fought to maintain a right teaching of the hope of the gospel.[8]
>
> Mark Dever

Save the Girl

There's a scene in the movie *The Book of Eli* when Denzel Washington, the hero, walks away from a girl being raped.

Every time I see that scene, my heart breaks. I want him to climb down the hill, kick some bad-guy butt, take the girl into his arms, and tell her she's okay.

But he walks away. The girl isn't his problem.

The body of Christ is in trouble, just like that girl. The church is beaten and bruised alongside the road. She's naked, dirty, an eyesore to believers and nonbelievers alike. Loving her is hard, but she is the love of our first love. Jesus Christ will never leave her nor forsake her. He will go to her, pick her up, and heal her.

We too must go to her.

We too must love her.

Over the past few years, I've been trying to help the girl. It didn't look pretty at first. But that's just it: Helping a hurt person is messy. There's no right way to do it. You just help because Jesus has shown

> Jesus said that this is how the world would know that we are his disciples, by the love we have for one another…Without this love we are nothing.[9]
>
> Mark Dever

you that no person should die of neglect—no matter what they've done.

Right now, there are thousands of churches that are hurting and maybe even dying. I urge you to commit yourself to doing the hard work of love in the body of Christ. To conquer your frustration, revive the dead and dying, and fall deeper in love with Jesus and his beautiful mess of a bride.

Having a longing to experience love, unity, and a deep hunger for Jesus is wonderful. But the church isn't meant to satisfy our longings. It's meant for messed-up believers to move *toward* love, unity, and a deep hunger for Jesus. If we're not moving toward these like Infiltrators do, then we're just part of the problem.

This book is about being a part of the solution. This book is about saving the girl.

Making the Most of This Book
Accomplish Points

Even if a chapter seems long, don't let that stop you from reading a few paragraphs. This book is written with numerous accomplish points per chapter: short blocks of text, bullet points, and quotes. These allow you to focus on compact ideas while also giving you the freedom to put the book down in a moment's notice without interrupting the flow.

Words You Can Put into Action

At the end of each chapter is a section called, "What Now?" Included in each of them are three elements: A link to the chapter's video, a free download of an important aspect covered in the material, and an invitation to connect with me on Facebook. Immediately after is a "What's Next" section, which offers a glimpse of what's to come in the next chapter.

CHAPTER 2

Why You Must Stay

If Any One of You Is Without Sin

Forget the title of this chapter. If your church doesn't desire God's presence or want to radiate his glory, leave. If your church doesn't care about the greatest commandments of love and the great commission to reach others, leave. If your church cares more about the building than the people, leave.

But before you do, read John 8:2-11:

> Early in the morning [Jesus] came again to the temple. All the people came to him, and he sat down and taught them. The scribes and the Pharisees brought a woman who had been caught in adultery, and placing her in the midst they said to him, "Teacher, this woman has been caught in the act of adultery. Now in the Law Moses commanded us to stone such women. So what do you say?" This they said to test him, that they might have some charge to bring against him. Jesus bent down and wrote with his finger on the ground. And as they continued to ask him, he stood up and said to them, "Let him who is without sin among you be the first to throw a stone at her." And once more he bent down and wrote on the ground. But when they heard it, they went away one by one, beginning with the older ones, and Jesus was left alone with the woman standing before him. Jesus stood up and said to her, "Woman, where are they? Has no one condemned you?" She said, "No one,

Lord." And Jesus said, "Neither do I condemn you; go, and from now on sin no more."

The church is guilty. She's gotten in bed with the world. Turned her back on Christ, her husband. We're justified in excommunicating her. We're justified in wanting better for Jesus. Right?

Thing is, according to Scripture, Jesus shows us that no, we're not.

As much as we want to stone the ungodliness in the church, Jesus simply signals us to calm down.

> From the Song of Solomon to the book of Revelation, the truth of Scripture is that Jesus loves his bride the Church. There's just no getting around it and we ought to stop trying.[1]
>
> Stephen Mansfield

"Wouldn't it be better to get rid of the filth, Jesus?" we question him as he bends to write in the sand. "We can do it right here, right now."

Then Jesus stands and says, "If any one of you is without sin…throw a stone at her."

As we try to process his words, wanting so badly to just throw the rock, we hear Jesus whisper to her: "Has no one condemned you?"

"No one," she responds.

"Then neither do I condemn you," Jesus says. "Go now and leave your life of sin."

This passage shows us that:

- We are not to condemn someone, no matter how messed up.
- We are to speak truth in love to unlovely people, no matter how difficult the circumstances.

Today, few of us are speaking truth in love to her because it's hard. This needs to change.

This is why we need Infiltrators.

Infiltration Is a Commandment

Let us consider how we may spur one another on toward love and good deeds, not giving up meeting together, as some are in the habit of doing, but encouraging one another—and all the more as you see the Day approaching (Hebrews 10:24-25 NIV).

Infiltration is a commandment, not an option.

No matter where we gather as the people of God, we are to think about how we can, in all encouragement, help our brothers and sisters embrace the radical call of following Jesus. And not just once in a while, but "all the more" as his return draws nearer.

> The solution begins from inside the church with the changing of God's people.[2]
>
> Ed Stetzer

Infiltration shocks those who, knowingly or unknowingly, embrace status-quo Christianity: those who decide they're in a good spot with God and have no more desire to grow in his ways. There is no church without status-quo believers. There are only churches with degrees of status-quo believers. In other words, infiltration can be practiced in any church.

The beauty of it is that infiltration doesn't require a big conference, social media momentum, or big budgets in order to work.

All it needs is you.

You Can Influence Thousands

> You are the light of the world. A city set on a hill cannot be hidden. Nor do people light a lamp and put it under a basket, but on a stand, and it gives light to all in the house. In the same way, let your light shine before others, so that they may see your good works and give glory to your Father who is in heaven (Matthew 5:14-16).

You have the power to influence—and it's greater than you think.

Everyone you know, everyone you meet, every person you come in contact with throughout the day—and everything that's said about you by anyone—translates into a ginormous influence. The question is, how are you using it?

Infiltration is about using your power and influence to the fullest inside the church. Imagine what would happen if your life mirrored the examples in Scripture.

- What might ignite if you desired transformation in your church and prayed for those who've neglected the true, simple call of Christ (Romans 10:1-4)? If you grieved for the state of your church and hoped to be used for its sake—even if it meant suffering severely for it (Romans 9:1-3)? If you focused on the fact that her blindness today is causing thousands of Christians to passionately cling to Christ all the more (Romans 11:11-12)?

> Without the impact on human beings, we are only playing church.[3]
>
> Ed Stetzer

- What might change if you desperately wanted your ministry to stir churches to the truth of Jesus (Romans 11:13-14)? If you crushed every last fiber of spiritual conceitedness inside yourself that makes you think you're better than people in the church (Romans 11:25-26)? If you met with the people in your church regularly, encouraged them, and prompted them to love others and do good deeds (Hebrews 10:24-25)?

- Would lukewarm believers turn red-hot if you infiltrated your church—and didn't sin even when you were angry with it (Ephesians 4:25-26)? If you bore them in love and made every effort to keep unity with them (Ephesians 4:1-3)? If you took your obligation to them—not just the unbelievers in your life—seriously (Romans 13:8-10)?

- Would Christ look attractive to the world if you carried the failings of your church and equipped yourself with the endurance of Christ (Romans 15:1-7)? If you devoted yourself to them in love, honoring others in your church above yourself (Romans 12:9-12)? If you lived in harmony with them, let go of pride, and associated yourself with believers of low spiritual position (Romans 12:16)?

- Would frustration and bitterness recede if you chose not to repay your church's evil for evil, but rather loved it in front of the world and did your best to live at peace with her people (Romans 12:17-18)? If you accepted weak believers in the church without quarreling with them over disputable matters (Romans 14:1-4)? If you refused to pass judgment on them or put stumbling blocks in their way (Romans 14:13)?

The only way we'll ever find out is if we infiltrate.

It's time for passionate lovers of Christ to make every effort in our churches to do what leads to peace and mutual edification, and refuse to destroy the work of God (Romans 14:19-20). It's time to put on tender mercies, kindness, humility, meekness, long-suffering, and bear one another's burdens, never ceasing to forgive each other (Colossians 3:12-14).

If we want to make a difference in this world, we must become Infiltrators of our churches.

Why You Must Infiltrate

> By this all people will know that you are my disciples, if you have love for one another (John 13:35).

Infiltrating teaches you how to love the unlovely. It drives you to not only study God's Word, but to *live out* his commands. It helps you and other believers gravitate toward Christlikeness. It shows you the great price Jesus suffered for the sake of wandering souls.

Most importantly, infiltrating ignites true Christian love into a flame not even a distracted world can ignore.

The sad part about infiltrating is that while many believers benefit from it, few pay it forward. Think for a moment about all of the godly influences you've had in your life. People who've played a part in your spiritual growth,

> You can unite with others in your church to put the world on notice by living God's Word together.[4]
>
> Ed Stetzer

held your hand through tough stretches, and inspired you to love people and do good works for King Jesus.

God used these believers to bring you to where you are today. They infiltrated your soul with passionate commitment to Jesus in spite of your immaturity, hardheadedness, or imbalance—and God caused you to grow. This is invaluable to you and your soul—and that's the point.

Infiltrating the church is invaluable to the souls of *others*—your brothers and sisters in Christ.

Investing in believers—no matter which spiritual stage they're in—is a massive part of the great commission. But rare is the believer who looks within his or her church and thinks, *Who do you want me to invest in, God?*

We cannot let this continue. We need to get busy infiltrating.

When You Infiltrate…
You Help Other Believers Become More Like Jesus

When we leave the church because people are fake, lukewarm, or stagnant, then we're leaving people who desperately need to see the way of Jesus. I used to be one of them.

Just like Jesus discipled the Twelve for three years, our fellow believers need someone to show them—just as the man in Acts 8:31 needed Phillip to show him—that Christ must be their first relationship, first purpose, and only true source of wealth.

Pastors should be the spiritual leaders in churches. But that truth doesn't cancel out our responsibility to point others to Jesus. Through words and deeds, we need to help fellow believers see the whole way of our Almighty God.

> So Philip ran to him and heard him reading Isaiah the prophet and asked, "Do you understand what you are reading?" And he said, "How can I, unless someone guides me?" And he invited Philip to come up and sit with him (Acts 8:30-31).

You Discover Others Who Long to Be More Like Jesus

One of the best parts of infiltrating is discovering others who share your innermost longing to live radically for Jesus. A lot of the time, they aren't who you might think.

Ever since I decided to live intentionally in my church, God's shown me just what a horrible evaluator I am of other believers. Those I'd profiled as status-quo Christians? They boiled with fire for Christ. Those I thought fit the description of head-but-no-heart believers? They were undergoing serious heart change.

This quickly taught me that I needed to get to know my fellow believers better—not judge their relationship with Jesus. I needed to talk with them. Have dinner with them. Laugh with them.

This is when God does amazing things in both of your lives.

There are so, so many people in church who want to live radically for Jesus. But they feel alone, outnumbered, and a little rebellious and ashamed. Infiltrators are the key to loosening their chains.

Freeing followers to a greater commitment is the Infiltrator's ultimate goal. But it's also a great privilege and awesomely fun.

Because when captives are set free, they go all sorts of crazy for Christ.

> I thank my God in all my remembrance of you, always in every prayer of mine for you all making my prayer with joy, because of your partnership in the gospel from the first day until now (Philippians 1:3-5).

You Bring Balance and Perspective to the Church

For years, people in my church made semi-frequent jokes about charismatic believers. They didn't mean any harm, but these quips subtly stirred disunity by making our less charismatic church seem "better" or more "mature." So I spoke up in love.

Don't get me wrong. I'm all for joking and keeping it real with believers of all denominations and backgrounds. But when it comes to things that stir spiritual snootiness or disunity? Not good.

Now it's been a long time since I've heard jokes about my charismatic brothers and sisters, whom I love dearly. A small change, some might say. But any time balance and perspective increases, the body of Christ wins.

> Finally, all of you, have unity of mind, sympathy, brotherly love, a tender heart, and a humble mind (1 Peter 3:8).

You Practice Great Forgiveness

To stay in a church, whether you've been deeply hurt or not, requires a lifestyle of forgiveness. Because you will wrong others and others will wrong you. This is the nature of imperfection.

And it's really a beautiful thing to be a part of.

If our ultimate goal is to be like Jesus, then forgiving the unforgivable is the biggest step to achieving it. In fact, we're never more like Christ than when we're forgiving someone who doesn't deserve it.

The proof is in the cross.

> Then Peter came up and said to him "Lord, how often will my brother sin against me, and I forgive him? As many as seven times?" Jesus said to him, "I do not say to you seven times, but seventy-seven times" (Matthew 18:21-22).

You Do Work for the Audience of One

We all want to make a difference in this world. But not just a difference. A big difference. The problem with this desire is that we often overlook the small differences we can make along the way. The differences seen by no one but God: the Audience of One.

Like discovering your gift and serving the body with it.

Or engaging in vulnerable and sometimes awkward discussions with other believers who are stuck in a spiritual rut.

We may be pretty good at drowning out our heart's compassion with large doses of television and ice cream, but deep down we want to be part of making a difference in others' lives.[5]

Ed Stetzer

This kind of work doesn't get noticed. It comes purely from a heart set on wanting to please Jesus—not the people around us.

Nothing is small to God when it's done in service to him. Infiltrators would all do well to take up the motto that *small is the new big.*

> But when you give to the needy, do not let your left hand know what your right hand is doing, so that your giving may be in secret. And your Father who sees in secret will reward you (Matthew 6:3-4).

You Gain Wisdom from Others

The foolish and ignorant think they're the most spiritual people in their churches. The wise, however, seek out those who exude a deep love for Jesus and wish to glean from them.

Chances are that many of your fellow believers are farther along in their walk with Christ—if not in knowledge, then in maturity, and if not in maturity, then in love (2 Peter 1:5-8). It's to your great advantage to listen to them and gain their wisdom.

That said, we're not supposed to soak in someone's words just because he or she is older than us or has been a lifetime believer. This is a big mistake I made growing up. Instead, listen to those who know God, love God, and do what God says. Don't assume there's no one like that in your church. Start diving into conversations with the people in the body, and you'll find them.

> Iron sharpens iron, and one man sharpens another (Proverbs 27:17).

You Make Jesus's Bride More Attractive to the World

Serving our brothers and sisters, loving them, and stirring them to a greater commitment to Jesus makes the church, the bride of Christ, more attractive to the world. And she needs that.

Not just to curb the stigma of judgmental Christians. But to stir up sentiments such as, "Wow, these people care about each other. These people love each other. These people would do anything for each other."

When an unbeliever starts asking what's different about us and our church, we know God has used infiltration to change hundreds, if not thousands, of lives.

But that moment doesn't come without the fight of a lifetime.

Right now, the world is amused by the church's self-destruction. It likes poking fun at her and exposing her warts. What's worse is that more and more *believers* are joining in the jeering, as if Christ has finally given up on his bride and now wants to stone her.

It's time to pour the energy it takes to criticize the church into loving the unlovely within her. Our goal shouldn't be to prove to the world that we're not messed up. It should be to prove that we're messed up but that God is sticking with us, slowly transforming our wicked hearts.

You Double Your Reach with the Gospel

We have amazing purpose and influence. We get to tell others about the one and only King who died so that we might live. We get to teach others about how Jesus wants us to love and serve his Father. We get to live our lives in complete and utter fearlessness because we have Christ.

But somewhere along the line, passionate followers of Christ decided that they were only going to tell some people about Jesus, and only teach some people about his ways. They'd restrict the message to people *outside* the church, because the ones inside were just too sick.

I understand the reasoning behind the decision. Ask any contractor and you'll discover that it's far easier to build new houses than it is to fix up crooked ones. But when contractors refuse to take on jobs of shoring up weak houses, they immediately neglect half of the people who need their skills.

Thing is, we're not talking about houses. We're talking about souls.

Infiltrators are the kind of contractors who not only build new houses, but specialize in shoring up old ones as well. They double their reach and guarantee that they'll never run out of work, even in a bad economy. Because even when few new houses are going up, there will always be old ones in need of restoration.

To ignore half of the people in spiritual need isn't God's plan. In a way, it's like refusing to take care of your own family—a prospect for which the Bible reserves harsh words.

> But if anyone does not provide for his relatives, and especially for members of his household, he has denied the faith and is worse than an unbeliever (1 Timothy 5:8).

You Live Out the Beatitudes

- Infiltrators must be humble to be effective. "Blessed are the poor in spirit, for theirs is the kingdom of heaven" (Matthew 5:3).

- Infiltrators must see their sin clearly and mourn over it before they can ever infiltrate. "Blessed are they who mourn, for they shall be comforted" (Matthew 5:4).

- Infiltrators must be gentle and kind, even in the sometimes hostile conditions of their churches. "Blessed are the meek, for they shall inherit the earth" (Matthew 5:5).

- Infiltrators must long to do justice and live right before God in their churches. "Blessed are they who hunger and thirst for righteousness, for they shall be satisfied" (Matthew 5:6).

- Infiltrators must be merciful as they patiently point others to Jesus in their churches. "Blessed are the merciful, for they shall obtain mercy" (Matthew 5:7).

- Infiltrators must desire to honor and worship God in everything they do in the church. "Blessed are the pure of heart, for they shall see God" (Matthew 5:8).

- Infiltrators must aim to stir up peace and unity among their brothers and sisters. "Blessed are the peacemakers, for they shall be called children of God" (Matthew 5:9).

- Infiltrators are persecuted for the sake of righteousness, not as martyrs, but by fellow believers who don't know any better. "Blessed are they who are persecuted for the sake of righteousness, for theirs is the Kingdom of Heaven" (Matthew 5:10).

You Overcome Church Messiness

Purge is an interesting word. In one sense, it's about getting rid of things that are undesirable. But in another sense, it's about purifying things that are dirty.

Leaving the church rids us of undesirable people. Infiltrating the church purifies dirty people.

The people in our churches are family. They're blood. They're brothers and sisters we're going to spend eternity with in heaven. There are lots of days when I wish I could get together with only fervent followers of Christ. But Jesus wants you and me to reach the sick, not the healthy. Sinners, not the righteous.

Even if those sinners are in the church.

In the book of Revelation, Jesus speaks to seven different churches (five of which are really messed up), affirming them for what is good, rebuking them for what is not, and lovingly calling them to turn from their wrongs and to *overcome*.

> The sad reality is that there are churches and church leaders that grossly misrepresent Jesus Christ through their lives and teaching. And you only need to attend one ineffective, unfriendly, or lethargic church to send all the soaring rhetoric about the bride of Christ falling to earth.[6]
>
> Joshua Harris

- To the church in Ephesus, Jesus speaks highly of the people's hard work, perseverance, and how they do not tolerate false teachers and doctrine, but rebukes them for abandoning their bleeding-heart zeal and the joy of when they first believed.

- To the church in Pergamum, he speaks highly of the people for staying true to the name of Jesus and not denying him in spite of terrible times of tragedy, but rebukes them for mixing doctrines and following wicked teachings of sexual immorality.

- To the church in Thyatira, he speaks highly of the people's ever-growing love, faith, and service, but rebukes them for tolerating the teachings of a seductive prophetess.

- To the church in Sardis, he only acknowledges that there are a few followers who have not "soiled their garments." He then rebukes them for being known as a church that's alive—when it's actually dead.

- To the church in Laodicea, he rebukes them for being neither hot nor cold in their faith, which he considers wretched, pitiful, poor, blind, and naked.

Churches are good in some areas, messed up in others, and God is calling us to overcome the messed-up stuff. The question is: Who's supposed to ignite this overcoming? Who's supposed to stand up and say, "We're missing it here"? Who's going to infuse the love and truth needed to overcome?

The answer is you. The answer is us.

I started my Christian walk as a Sardis/Laodicea believer, you might say. But God sent Jesus-loving people into my life who absolutely rocked my world with passionate commitment, flipping my noisy-gong heart upside-down.

The cool thing is that most of them didn't even know they were having an influence on me. They just seamlessly infiltrated my soul with Jesus. Brought me face-to-face with the fact that I was a dead Christian who knew the Bible but didn't truly follow Christ. Without their grueling, thankless, nobody-sees-it-but-God infiltration, I'd still be a loveless wretch today. But now I am crazy for my savior, and I will pay my infiltration forward.

What about you?

> Do not be overcome by evil, but overcome evil with good (Romans 12:21).

You Fulfill a Forgotten Part of the Great Commission

We often hear about going and making disciples of all nations, whether that means telling our neighbor about Jesus or taking the Word to a village in Zimbabwe. What we don't hear often is that we are supposed to teach people to "observe [obey] all that I have commanded you" (Matthew 28:20).

This is a never-ending process, and the church is in desperate need of believers who are willing to give their lives to it.

Baptizing new believers is a one-time event. Teaching them to obey all that Jesus has commanded is a lifetime event. One part of the process is not easier or better than another. They're just different aspects of the process God uses to adopt lost sinners into his family.

> He who loves his dream of a community more than the Christian community itself becomes a destroyer of the latter, even though his personal intentions may be ever so honest and earnest and sacrificial.[7]
>
> Dietrich Bonhoeffer

> And Jesus came and said to them, "All authority in heaven and on earth has been given to me. Go therefore and make disciples of all nations, baptizing them in the name of the Father and of the Son and of the Holy Spirit, teaching them to observe all that I have commanded you. And behold, I am with you always, to the end of the age" (Matthew 28:18-20).

> Think of a family. Whenever your parents, siblings, or children fail to meet your expectations, do you suddenly throw them out of the family?[8]
>
> Mark Dever

You Avoid the Spiritual Runaround

Tyson couldn't stand his family. They were screwed up. They were embarrassing. They didn't live their lives the way normal people did. So he left, deciding that if no one else was going to do life right, he would.

It was scary at first, but getting away from his crazy family was exhilarating. Tyson felt free. He felt real. He felt true to himself and to the life he was supposed to live.

But after a while, the thrill wore off and he felt...lonely. He got angry with his old family because he knew that if they had just lived the way they were supposed to, that they could still be together.

Tyson decided that the best solution was to start a family of his own. So he got married, had children, and started befriending people who he thought were living their lives as normal people do. Everything was wonderful.

But, after some time, a few of his new relatives and their families started doing weird, embarrassing things. They stopped living the way they were supposed to.

Tyson did his best to talk sense into them, but it didn't do any good. The way he thought life should be lived and the way they thought life should be lived, though similar, was different. There was nothing that could be done.

> On a sad note, we really do have favorites, and normally they are people like us. Jesus has no favorites. He loves everyone with a lavish, everlasting love. Even those we consider high maintenance or emotionally unhealthy.[9]
>
> Ed Stetzer

As Tyson's children grew older, they too got tired of their family's weird, embarrassing ways of living. It broke Tyson's heart. He tried pleading and reasoning with his children, but it was no good. They grew old enough to leave Tyson's family altogether.

They wanted to live their lives the way *they* thought was normal.

Spiritual Runaround

Tyson is like the person who leaves the church. First, it's scary. Then it's thrilling. Then lonely.

This loneliness eventually leads to a sort of nontraditional, solo way of following Jesus that doesn't adhere to what we see in the New Testament. Not only that, but solo followers tend to be pretty vocal about their disdain for the church, slandering her via the Internet and social avenues, or quietly speaking badly of her—both of which are extremely harmful to God's people.

If loneliness becomes too much for the solo follower, he usually finds and befriends other believers who share his likes and theology, or he begins a house church or small community of believers.

These communities can be awesome—gatherings where you can

find real authenticity and a longing to follow Jesus, do justice, love mercy, walk humbly, and go into the world to make disciples. But, as good as these small groups of believers can be, they eventually run into one of two problems:

They either refuse to let others into the inner circle who don't think and live like they do (i.e., getting rid of the filth). Or else they accept every believer who comes along and eventually face the same questions that led to the creation of churches and denominations as we know them today:

- Where might be a place we can meet regularly? When is the best time to meet? How should we celebrate the Lord's Supper and baptism—or should we do them at all?

- Doesn't Scripture imply that we should have a pastor, elders, and deacons? Should we have some sort of membership?

- What if one of the group sins big-time? Do we just forgive and move on, or do we practice church discipline? Who makes the final decision when there is disagreement?

- Who's going to be there for the needier people in the group?

- What do we do when one of the group interprets Scripture differently from the rest of the group, especially on core issues?

- Should children come to the meetings? If not, who's going to watch them? What about the electric bill? Who should handle the money side of things?

Churchless groups of believers either suppress those who have beliefs and ideas that are different from theirs (just like traditional churches) or they grow in numbers and diversity until a building and structure is absolutely needed to survive (just like traditional churches).

In other words, those who leave the church in order to be the church end up needing a church.

If local churches just went away, we'd all start building new ones.

Because we need authority and roles to survive. Apart from structure, people fail. Just imagine a busy airport's security line without those roped-off lanes. No one would take off without the organization implemented.

Positives definitely arise out of the grassroots church experience, but at the end of the day, it's kind of a spiritual runaround.

Infiltration is different.

Infiltrators infuse the love and truth of Jesus—the very ingredients that transform messy people—into already existing structures. The time to stay in church is now. We're already promised success. But God's given us the responsibility to love the church, forgive her, and give our lives to her.

> Therefore be imitators of God, as beloved children. And walk in love, as Christ loved us and gave himself up for us, a fragrant offering and sacrifice to God (Ephesians 5:1-2).

You Embrace God's Plan for Church Structure

Wherever the body of Christ meets is called church, and it can be anywhere. But the Bible clearly calls for structure and membership because without it, we crumble.

- God wants pastors, elders, and deacons, and he wants us to devote ourselves to their teaching—even if it's longer than 20 minutes (Ephesians 4:11-12, Acts 2:42). Sometimes leading the church becomes such a full-time job that they must appoint others to take care of the physical needs of the church (Acts 6:1-7).

- God wants us to respect, submit to, and show confidence in our authorities in the church, who watch over our souls and must give an account for doing so (1 Thessalonians 5:12; Hebrews 13:17).

- God wants us to "come together as a church" and have some sort of membership in local churches (1 Corinthians

11:18). He wants us joined to something: the church (Acts 14:21-23), the body of Christ (1 Corinthians 12:27). Otherwise, there'd be no grounds for the commands of church discipline (1 Timothy 5:19-20).

- God wants us to "behave in the household of God, which is the church of the living God, a pillar and buttress of the truth" (1 Timothy 3:15). He wants us to do all things "decently and in order" in the church (1 Corinthians 14:40). He wants us to partake in the Lord's Supper (1 Corinthians 11:26), pray (Acts 2:42), baptize (Matthew 28:19), sing spiritual songs (Ephesians 5:19), and read Scripture (1 Timothy 4:13).

- God wants us to practice our spiritual gifts to serve others as faithful stewards of his grace in its various forms, speaking as those who speak the very words of God, and serving as through his strength alone (1 Peter 4:10; Romans 12:6-8; 1 Corinthians 12:4-11).

> So while the Bible doesn't provide us with a biblical treatise on membership per se, there is enough evidence in the inspired record to suggest that some form of membership was practiced and was necessary to the church's operation.[10]
>
> Thabiti M. Anyabwile

This structure—in traditional churches, tent churches, house churches—leads to funded missionaries, wells dug, people loved, kids cared for, and so much more. In spite of sinful people, the work is getting done.

And yet it's all the sinful people in churches that hold us back from participation. These sinful people are just going through the motions, we think. But are they? Or are they actually becoming more like Jesus?

The job infiltrators play is helping those just going through the motions move closer to Christ.

You Invite God to Work in Your Soul

It's been said that there's mean, and then there's "church people" mean. The apostle Paul had to deal with church people mean.

But he didn't just deal with them. He loved them.

In 1 Corinthians 4:9 we read that Paul and the other apostles are like "men sentenced to death, because we have become a spectacle to the world, to angels, and to men." I can't help but wonder if they were considered spectacles because they were ripped not only by unbelievers, but believers as well.

I mean, Paul wrote tear-filled letters to church people who would come to communion drunk. He even had to prove to them that he wasn't a fraud.

A spectacle indeed...except to God.

To infiltrate a church is to get some flack, either subtly or overtly, from people inside. But it's in this hardship that God does serious work on your soul, teaching you to depend on his power to speak, his power to love, his power to overlook offenses, and his power to forgive.

God makes us more like Jesus through infiltration. He shows us what it means to lay down our lives for his sheep. It's not easy, and we may never stop experiencing doubts. But this is the beauty of our call to love God and love others.

Experiencing doubt, weakness, and ineptitude while infiltrating is not a warning that we're doing something wrong. They're confirmation that we're doing something right. They show us that we're no longer consuming church, but loving her and speaking truth to her even when it's hard.

> Count it all joy, my brothers, when you meet trials of various kinds, for you know that the testing of your faith produces steadfastness. And let steadfastness have its full effect, that you may be perfect and complete, lacking in nothing (James 1:2-4).

You Are Equipped

Infiltration is for everyone. But there are some believers who face fewer roadblocks while infiltrating.

If you are a *Frustrated* or a *Sieged*, and if you're anywhere from your late teens to thirties, then you are in the best position to infiltrate.

- You have the passion and energy to go full-throttle in spite of various trials.

- You have a deep desire to be a part of something meaning-ful, difference-making, and challenging—not just for a time, but for the rest of your life.

- You are equipped to infiltrate through every avenue of technology, including all kinds of social media and its far-reaching waves.

- You have the infrastructure to not only infiltrate your home church, but to connect with other Infiltrators all over the world.

- You are being observed by the whole of Christianity, and your infiltration is a statement that while the church doesn't have to worry about you leaving, it does have to worry about your radical desire to follow the way of Jesus.

- You have the support of so many believers who want to see you stay in church and watch your relationship with Jesus grow.

- You probably do not have a position in the church that someone may use against you as you infiltrate.

I wasn't always amped up about staying in church. I wanted to leave mine for months and be a part of something bigger, something risk-ier, something all-in for Christ. But God wouldn't let me. Through his Spirit, I kept hearing a simple message: *Stay.*

Now I know why.

I stayed to glorify God by pushing myself and others to the unity, depth, and passion Jesus commands of us. That's it. No fancy mission. No frothing rebellion. Just *stay* and infiltrate.

Sometimes I sweat over whether or not I'm doing it right. Sometimes I feel less involved than I should, writing too much and living too little. Sometimes the last thing I want to do is say something gospel-related that I know will make others feel uncomfortable.

But God is patient with my failures and continues blessing me.

When my head is hanging, he lifts it up. When I need encouragement, he gives it. When I need a kick to get in motion, he obliges through various means. When pride rears its ugly face, he punches it quickly.

If there's one thing I've learned through infiltration, it's that God truly won't ever leave you or forsake you.

> Let no one despise you for your youth, but set the believers an example in speech, in conduct, in love, in faith, in purity (1 Timothy 4:12).

Profile of an Infiltrator

So what does an Infiltrator do?

> Churches say they have the best and most important news in the world…yet churches are made up of people like you and me, people who are grumpy, irritable, unfaithful, and selfish… We talk of love, but we too often give ourselves over to hate.[11]
>
> Mark Dever

- Infiltrators stir up a greater commitment to Jesus in the body of Christ. They stand for Jesus and his commands at the risk of their appearance and reputation. They are an integral piece in the plan God is orchestrating in the church.

- Infiltrators concern themselves with how they're living for Jesus before ever considering how others are living for him. They value the wisdom of believers who've gone before them and consider everything people say. They desire to sharpen and be sharpened, even if sparks are a part of the process.

- Infiltrators don't search for an ideal church. They live as though they are a part of an ideal church. They take the first step, knowing what the church can be if, one by one, her people start reflecting Christ.

- Infiltrators assess spiritual habits that are toxic in their church and then zero in on those things that are keeping the body from fully glorifying Jesus. Their focus is to speak directly into the things that plague her. They help move the shallow to authentic, the heady to the heart, the fearful to true faith.

- Infiltrators look to add value in the lives of others. They lay down their wants and desires to help their brothers and sisters discover the joy of what Jesus calls the "abundant life." Their agenda is to be used in the growth of other believers and to set the captives free. They look to serve others instead of being served.

The 3 Ways of an Infiltrator

Unity

Treat others in the church like family. Learn first names and call other believers "brother" or "sister." Embrace diversity, appreciate generational differences, and consider everyone in your church as more important than yourself.

Encourage other believers to love people and to do good things for unbelievers and believers alike. Look around your church and ask yourself how you can use your gifts to help others, not expecting anything in return.

Make friends with Christians of diverse backgrounds and denominations. Speak highly of other churches and pray for Jesus to do great work through them. Discourage your fellow believers from making other churches sound inferior and be quick to let go of offenses to your own.

Consider yourself bound to all believers in the great purpose of serving Jesus. Make secondary beliefs secondary, refusing to let non-essential opinions cut you off from fellowship. Love other believers whether or not they agree with you on gray areas of Scripture.

Meet others where they are and speak openly of your faults and imbalances. Aim to bring all believers together in unity, not *uniformity*, in which everyone looks the same and talks the same.

Depth

Don't overlook the difficulties and intricacies of Scripture in your calling to radically follow Jesus. And don't let those same difficulties and intricacies choke your calling to love God and others. Live your life in beautiful tension, subtly inviting others to do the same.

Be committed to a real relationship with Jesus. Don't look to fit him into your schedule, but fit your schedule around him. Think more about how to live like Jesus in real life than you do about theoretically living like him.

Don't desire to transfer your convictions into other believers. Simply make it your goal to help others live out the uncomplicated gospel of loving God, loving others, doing justice, loving mercy, and walking humbly.

Draw uptight believers into deeper levels of authenticity. Practice hospitality and true fellowship that centers on realness, truth, and love. Encourage your brothers and sisters on a very personal level, and listen not only for what's said on the surface, but also what's said underneath.

Explore hard questions that others won't—but refuse to fall into endless arguments and debates. Only say things that fit the occasion and build others up. Refuse to shift topics just so you can say what you want to say.

Do not shy away from speaking directly to the evils that sneak into your church. Openly speak against lukewarmness, head knowledge, pharisaical living, Christian snobbery, spiritual laziness, pride, conditional love, borrowed faith, consumerism, judgmentalism, cynicism, and grieving the Holy Spirit. Like the Bereans in Acts, cross-check what your fellow believers say, and speak up with grace when half truths are taught as full truths, or parts of the Bible are never spoken of.

Purpose

Look at the book of Acts and observe believers united in something so much greater than themselves. See believers living in unity and passion as though Jesus *actually* lives, and desperately want that for your church.

Go to church with an anticipation of worshipping God and glorying in his presence. Speak freely about heaven and what it will be like spending eternity with Jesus. Help others in your church see that there is so much more to the body than organization and institution. Your church is a mission, a movement, a calling.

Share the contagious stories God has orchestrated in your life. Retell stories of crazy faith, abandoned love, and seemingly unexplainable acts of God—viral stories that scream *God is real, God loves his children, and God has a great purpose for our lives.*

Invest time and energy into discovering and using the gifts and passions God has given you. Get to know your strengths and weaknesses, and put them to use in ways that push the boundaries of your own comfort. Use your gifts liberally for the body of Christ, help others discover their gifts, and aim to build God's church through your church.

Value love above all else, and make it the rhyme and rhythm of your life.

Be an Infiltrator.

Choose Their Good over Your Own

In Philippians 1, Paul, who's suffering in prison, says he wants to die but knows that it will be more profitable for the church if he stays. So he stays for the progress and joy of believers.

He chooses their good over his own.

Our brothers and sisters need us, and we need them. The less mature among us need the more mature. The less Jesus-filled need the more Jesus-filled. Our churches need Infiltrators willing to do things and say things that subtly shake souls, stir minds, and create amazing opportunities for the Holy Spirit to infuse intense affection for Jesus.

Be that person. Infiltrate the brother who gets on your nerves. Infiltrate the sister who's weak in faith or lacking in spiritual strength. Say what needs to be said. Do what needs to be done. Build up your fellow believers regardless of their messiness, "for this is the will of God in Christ Jesus for you" (1 Thessalonians 5:14-18).

> The exclusion of the weak and insignificant, the seemingly useless people, from a Christian community may actually mean the exclusion of Christ; in the poor brother Christ is knocking at the door. We must, therefore, be very careful.[12]
>
> Dietrich Bonhoeffer

Paul tells us to run the race to win. But running to win isn't about passing everybody. True heroes on the track are the ones who give up their shot at a medal to pick up a runner who's fallen bloody on the track and carry them to the finish line.

Last place, as Jesus tells us, is truly first place.

> Do nothing from rivalry or conceit, but in humility count others more significant than yourselves (Philippians 2:3).

What Now?

Watch this chapter's video at www.calledtostay.com.

Get the download of "Profile of an Infiltrator" at www.calledtostay.com.

"An Infiltrator of the church is someone who…" — Post this as your Facebook status and I'll join the conversation (just remember to tag me).

What's Next

As it is with most new concepts, there is no shortage of questions about infiltrating. In the next chapter, we'll hit some of those questions.

CHAPTER 3

Infiltrating Q & A

What About Those Saying I Should Leave the Church?

There are a lot of opinions out there about staying in church or leaving the church. Some say that the exodus is the Holy Spirit at work, cleansing us from religious gunk. Some say that leaving the church is like leaving your home—it's just a scary part of life that helps you grow as a person.

I understand these points of views and the reasoning behind them. But what I don't understand is their biblical support. Because I can't find Scripture that supports them.

I'm not against innovative thinking or examining the way we live and ought to follow Jesus. But when someone builds a leave-the-church thesis that questions the authority of the Bible or steps outside its clearly marked guides, God is not pleased.

The reality that it's not always pretty living in communion with other believers in no way gives us the right to pronounce the plans of the Holy Spirit or finagle Scripture to make it sound like we've gotten God wrong for hundreds of years.

When in doubt about staying in or leaving the church, go to Scripture and see what God says about his bride.

How Do Infiltrators Keep from Burning Out?

One of the most important things Infiltrators need to remember is to focus on intentionality, not results.

Missionaries are a great example of intentionality. Sometimes they pour their lives and souls into a foreign people but never have the privilege of seeing any of them give their lives to Christ.

But the seed is planted. Ready for water. And ready, ultimately, for the growth God gives.

Like marriage, intentionality is all about giving 100 percent no matter how much the other gives you back. It's not easy to do. It's not natural. But that's what God calls us to. The good news is that he equips us to do it.

Focusing on intentionality is saying and doing things with a planned purpose, such as...

- Taking conversations to a deeper level by asking people about their relationship with God and what he's been teaching them. Sincerely ask them, "How's your heart?"

- Inviting people over for lunch or dinner to really talk and get real.

- Asking questions whenever something seems off.

- Challenging those who practice "safe" Christianity.

- Speaking up whenever someone teaches a gray area of the Bible as black and white.

Focusing on intentionality keeps you sane and purposeful. It keeps you doing what you can, whenever you can, for as many people as you can. It's doing what you can control in any given moment.

The moment you stop focusing on intentionality and start focusing on results is the moment you'll get down. Because infiltration isn't about changing people. It's about letting God use you in the growth of others. We do what we can in the operating room while God performs open-heart surgery.

Focus on intentionality, not results.

Turn Frustration into Fuel

Church not involved in community service projects?
Start one and invite others to participate.

Not getting the care and love you feel you need?
Give care and love to others.

Not getting fed? Start feeding yourself.

No genuine fellowship? Create genuine fellowship.

Holding on to grudges? Let go and exude amazing grace.

Weighed down by church hurt? Cast your cares on Jesus.

Church consumed by appearance?
Seek to amplify Jesus in every way possible.

Shallow fellowship?
Take people into deeper levels of authenticity a little at a time.

Wouldn't Jesus Turn over Tables in Most Churches?

Jesus doesn't like a ton of what happens (and doesn't happen) in his church. Matthew 21:12-13 tells the story of what happened when Jesus visited the temple and discovered it filled with people buying and selling. They were maliciously using God for personal gain, so Jesus came in and let his righteous fury loose. He said, "It is written, 'My house shall be called a house of prayer,' but you make it a den of robbers."

The question is…does this justify us to leave most churches today?

No, it doesn't. Not because of what I say, but because of what God has shown us.

If your church is using God for personal profit, that's one thing. Turn the tables and leave. But if you look to the Bible, you'll see that for every group of people that would drive Jesus to turn tables, there are many more to which Jesus would start speaking the truth in love.

God doesn't give us many reasons to turn tables. What he does give are countless examples of loving unlovely people.

Isn't the Idea of Infiltration Prideful?

The idea of infiltration is to rise to the radical call of following Jesus within our churches and, in doing so, giving others permission to do so as well. So in that sense, no. It's not prideful.

But yes, pride is the big killer of Infiltrators.

- If someone stays in the church just to show others how tight they are with Jesus, *fail.*

- If someone stays in church just to lovelessly challenge everything in the church, *fail.*

- If someone stays in church looking to teach others without first being doubly teachable, *fail.*

- If someone dishes out love and truth only to grow inwardly bitter because they're the ones having to take the high road, *fail.*

Infiltration *is* pride if it's not done with humble childlikeness. So if you're put off by the idea, don't discard it until you've read that section.

When accompanied by self-examination, childlikeness, and the power of God inside us, infiltration is the farthest thing from pride you'll find. To infiltrate is to choose a thankless and often difficult road. But the difference it makes in the body of Christ is profound.

Are You Against All Alternative Churches?

Nothing could be further from the truth.

It's not that alternative churches are doing something wrong. It's that they do something wonderfully right in a way that's not sustainable.

Some alternative church environments are beautiful and awesome, filled with moments where you actually think to yourself that you're living like a true Christian. The group has one another's backs. People actually know each other. The homeless are fed and the widows and orphans cared for. Conversations are intimate and real.

But things that thrive, grow. And with growth comes diversity of thought and opinions. And with diversity of thought and opinions, conflict. And with conflict, hard decisions.

Like renting a building to meet in and filling the roles of pastor, elder, and deacon.

God lays out the structure and backbone needed for the body of Christ to excel. And, just as many churches adhere to proper structure but lack true Christianity, most alternative Christian environments don't have proper structure in spite of amazing hearts for God.

No, not all alternative churches are going in a spiritual runaround. Some of the strongest churches probably began with proper structure while meeting in homes. But even though God is most interested in our hearts, he doesn't want us to neglect his commands of structure.

What If a Church Doesn't Have One Real Christian in It?

My gut response is *run*. Because that is one messed-up church. Why throw pearls before swine?

But my rational response is *remember*.

- First, remember that while we can look for visible signs that someone is a believer, every Christian is in the process of growing from infancy to adulthood. No one can ever truly know the state of another's soul except God. So be slow to judge a church as having no true believers.

- Second, remember that God promised to spare Sodom and Gomorrah if only *ten* righteous people were found in them. He cares deeply for his own, even if they're the radical minority and surrounded by evil. This doesn't mean you should go plug into a rotten church. It means we shouldn't ignore infiltrating churches just because they're worse off than others.

- Third, remember the churches in Revelation. There is a church that's lost its zeal. A church that mixes doctrines and is sexually immoral. A church that tolerates the teachings of a heretic. A church that's "dead." And there's a lukewarm church that Jesus considers wretched and pitiful. Yet even in all of this sickness, he commends the churches for several different things and calls them to overcome their sinful ways.

Remember that if God doesn't write off churches easily, neither should we.

Isn't Infiltration Idealistic? Have You Ever Seen It Work?

Yes.

My wife and I almost left our home church before God clearly told us to stay. That's when he started teaching us what we now know as infiltration.

I started waking up on Sundays focusing on three things: unity, depth, and purpose.

- Unity, because for far too long I'd distanced myself from my brothers and sisters who didn't seem passionately committed to Jesus.

- Depth, because for far too long I never made an effort to invest in deep conversations with those in my church about God and life.

- Purpose, because for far too long I conformed to what I *thought* my church's purpose was instead of just living what God's purpose was.

When someone talked down about other Christians or denominations, I gently spoke up about our calling of love and unity. When opportunities arose to talk with someone after church, I aimed to take the conversation toward Jesus and doing life in light of him. When God moved me to spontaneously gush about him and his purpose for the body of Christ, I didn't hold back.

> You have the power to help create the irresistible church you long to be a part of.[1]
>
> Wayne Cordeiro

And when I had the opportunity to teach or lead, I'd go straight for the questions and subjects that would speak directly into our church's greatest weaknesses.

I didn't know what God was up to until I started seeing how infiltration both opened people's eyes to greater commitment and freed them from suppressing it. He slowly revealed the subtle but profound difference one of us can make by being intentional in the body of Christ.

None of these things are gold stars for me. They're simply things I aspire to—and often fail at.

The point of infiltration is not to do it without sin or error. The point is to do your best for Jesus while stirring up others to greater commitment to him.

Do You Know How People Would React If I Spoke Up Against My Church?

I should clarify what I mean. Speaking against your church's flaws isn't about slandering the church and always saying that the church is lukewarm, or spiritually lazy, or prideful, or cynical, or grieving the Holy Spirit. Not at all.

To infiltrate your church requires that you first assess what its weaknesses seem to be and secondly, that you intentionally confront those weaknesses with the Bible. But this confronting isn't done through condemning what's wrong. It's done through camping on Scripture that just isn't manifesting itself in the church. It's done through constantly encouraging the body of Christ to rise to the way of Jesus.

- If your church operates more from head knowledge, focus on the heart.

- If your church puts a lot of emphasis on outward appearance, focus on deep within the human soul.

- If your church talks the talk, focus on walking the walk.

- If your church is proud, focus on humility.

- If your church soaks up sermons and worship without experiencing life-change, focus on the transformation of those who've truly encountered Jesus.

- If your church speaks a lot about God the Father and God

the Son but rarely mentions or explains the Holy Spirit, focus on the work of the third person of the Trinity.

- If your church is overprotective and cares more about what it doesn't do than what it does do, focus on the commands of Jesus that focus on doing.

- If your church is teaching a watered-down, wimpy version of the Bible, focus on the deep and radical life Jesus calls us to live.

- If your church dismisses science and difficult questions about God and his Word, focus on calling others to study Scripture holistically in faith, not fear—as though it had answers to every part of life.

Quietly, gradually. This is infiltration.

Take a moment and think about your church. What areas do you look at and think, "We're missing it here"? Does Scripture support your observation? How might you challenge this shortcoming in your church in a gentle, loving, and encouraging way?

> We have both an individual and a corporate responsibility to develop the churches we're part of.[2]
>
> Wayne Cordeiro

Is Infiltrating a Church Really Better Than Following Jesus Without the Church?

Sometimes we're confronted with a faulty ultimatum: that we must leave the church to truly follow Jesus…or else stay in church and be a part of the problem.

That is just not true.

Infiltration is one of the ways God causes believers to grow to full maturity in Christ. But following Jesus inside the church is an option no one wants to embrace because it's too difficult.

It's been said that discipline is the difference between what we want now (changes in our church) and what we want most (to radically follow Jesus). The problem is when we buy into believing that what we want now conflicts with what we *need* most.

Following Jesus and staying in church are not at odds with each other. They go hand-in-hand…and we're commanded to do both.

What Now?

"My question about infiltrating the church is…" — Post this as your Facebook status and I'll join the conversation (just remember to tag me).

What's Next

Deciding to stay and infiltrate the church is little more than a decision if you're not equipped and ready. The next section is the first step to making you ready.

PART 2

If You Want to Serve Your Savior

CHAPTER 4

Where to Start

The Most Important Question About Your Life

> You hypocrite, first take the log out of your own eye, and then you will see clearly to take the speck out of your brother's eye (Matthew 7:5).

You're sitting in front of the largest grand jury in the world. You don't know why you're here, but you get the sense that the rest of your life hinges on what's about to happen.

Everyone you've ever loved fills the seats in front of you: family, friends, romantic interests. You can see that they all care for you, but it's as if they're all holding their breath.

Finally, the lawyer approaches.

"I have a question for you." The lawyer points his finger at random people throughout the courtroom. "Look around. All these people have poured some part of themselves into you. They love you. They've probably spent countless hours with you, served you, hugged you, praised you, and given you gifts. There are probably many here who'd even take a bullet for you."

The lawyer turns toward a door on the left, where a man is escorted into the courtroom. Though you've never seen the man in person before, you recognize him immediately. Jesus.

"My question to you is simple," the lawyer says. "Can you, right now, in front of this grand jury and everyone you've ever loved, look this

man directly in the eyes and tell him—with life-or-death conviction—
that you love him with all of your heart, and all of your soul, and all
of your mind, and more than your father, and more than your mother,
and more than your family, and more than your friends? *Really?*

"Don't answer in haste," the lawyer warns. "Many fool themselves
into thinking that they love this Jesus more than anything and any-
body. But does your life reflect it? Do you spend time with him? Do
you hug him? Do you praise him? Do you serve him? Do you give him
gifts?" The lawyer glances at the onlookers, then back at you. "Until
you're ready to answer, this courtroom is adjourned."

If we are not one thousand percent sure that we love Jesus more
than everything and everybody in our lives, then we are not fit for
infiltration.

Let me ask you:

- When you get the opportunity to talk about Jesus, do you
  gush about your love for him or get emotional talking
  about him (Psalm 18:1-2)? Are you affectionate for him,
  prone to spontaneous boasts about Jesus for all that he is
  and all that he's done? Are you moved by the words he's
  penned for you (Psalm 119:97)? Are his ways written on
  your heart and mind (Hebrews 10:16)?

- Do you gaze at his beauty and let your love spring up from
  your soul (Psalm 27:4)? Do you go about your day seeing
  him and hearing him in the world around you? Are your
  prayers mere formulas, or do they burst from a place so
  deep that you're not even sure what might come out?

- Do you treasure God to the point that everything else
  just seems meaningless because you have him (Matthew
  13:44)? Is knowing Jesus the greatest thing that's ever happened to you (Philippians 3:8)? Do you dwell on his loving-
  kindness and praise him for all he's done for you (Isaiah
  63:7)? Can you say to your boyfriend, girlfriend, husband,
  or wife that you love God…even more than them?

- Do you get lost in God's unsearchable riches (Ephesians 3:8)? When you're worshipping, do you pour your heart and soul out to him, or are you embarrassed to truly humble yourself before him (1 Chronicles 29:20)? Do you ever find yourself singing to him from your deepest emotions, or playing an instrument for him from your innermost passion?

This is loving God with all of your heart and all of your soul and all of your mind. This is crying out "Abba, Father!"

Of course, Jesus doesn't only call us to love God with our mind and emotions, but also with our actions. Following him isn't just about feeling love for him. It's also about doing what he tells us to do. This requires digging deep.

Digging deep is to…

1. honestly assess how your life reflects the commands of Jesus

2. allow your heart to break where it needs breaking

3. pray for restoration

Those who dig deep don't do so by accident. It takes effort and intentionality. Because, honestly, it's not the most thrilling thing to do. It puts you face-to-face with areas of your spiritual walk in which you may be failing.

> If my sinfulness appears to me to be in any way smaller or less detestable in comparison with the sins of others, I am still not recognizing my sinfulness at all.[1]
>
> Dietrich Bonhoeffer

But the beautiful result of digging deep is an experience far too beautiful for any believer to miss. It's a must for every Infiltrator.

Why You Must Dig Deep
Digging Deep Precedes Rising Up

> The Lord lifts up the humble; he casts the wicked to the ground (Psalm 147:6).

The act of digging deep takes great humility. Because you have to get real with yourself. You have to take ownership of your lack of devotion to Jesus. It's hard. It hurts.

But if there's one thing that draws God's gaze, it's humility. God says his grace drenches the humble. He makes his home with the lowly. He takes time to guide and teach the humble. He exalts those who are humble. He gives salvation to the humble.

God. Loves. The. Humble.

And not only that. James 4:10 (NIV) says, "Humble yourselves before the Lord, and he will lift you up." In other words, digging deep precedes rising up. The problem is that few are willing to embrace true humility.

I think most of us would like to be another Moses, leading people out of captivity. I think most of us would like to be another David, a man after God's own heart. I think most of us, if given the choice, would clamor to be one of Jesus's disciples.

> Humility keeps us on track. It prevents us from adopting the faulty perspective that church is all about us.[2]
>
> Wayne Cordeiro

But would we like to have a stuttering problem? Would we like being the wimpy runt of a family? Would we choose to be illiterate fishermen?

Humility isn't just about directing praise to God after someone has praised you. It's about digging deep into your relationship with Jesus when no one is looking.

This is the way of digging deep, and Infiltrators must choose it.

Digging Deep Shows You How You Must Pray

> Watch and pray that you may not enter into temptation. The spirit indeed is willing, but the flesh is weak (Matthew 26:41).

Even though we are fearfully and wonderfully made, we are capable of great deceit and wickedness. Digging deep helps us see our greatest struggles and know exactly what we must pray about.

I don't mean prayer that, like a nursery rhyme, goes "Dear Jesus, help me do better in all areas of my life." I mean fervent prayer that pounds on heaven's door because you know that God alone has the power to change you. And that God alone responds to desperate hearts.

Infiltrators cannot be mediocre in prayer.

Jesus tells us to watch and pray. He says if his words remain in us that we may ask any request we like—and it will be granted according to his will. He tells us to pray all kinds of prayers and requests and to do so all the time. He says he hears the cry of the righteous and delivers them, and that "the prayer of a righteous person has great power as it is working" (James 5:16).

Chances are that you probably got sick of yourself sometime in the past month. You did something stupid, hurt God, and hated yourself for it. But when was the last time you thought, *I hate this about myself and I'm going to do something about it by letting God do something about it?* That is the power of prayer.

Infiltrators must embrace authentic prayer if we truly desire to be more like Jesus and have an influence in the body of Christ.

> If we work on ourselves harder than we work on the church, then the church becomes an automatic beneficiary... You follow Christ. You live with passion and calling. Throw your heart into your sphere of influence.[3]
>
> Wayne Cordeiro

Digging Deep Forces You to Examine Your Motives

> Search me, O God, and know my heart! Try me and know my thoughts! And see if there be any grievous way in me, and lead me in the way everlasting! (Psalm 139:23-24).

> "We'll show them!" has never been a biblical or an effective mission statement.[4]
>
> Ed Stetzer

When it comes to our innermost motives, many of us play the part of the ignorant parent, always thinking the child is great but looking the other direction when the kiddo is misbehaving.

Motive is the story behind why we do

things. To infiltrate successfully, you need to examine your motive as if everything else depended on it. Because everything else *does* depend on it.

If your motive is anything less than a desperate longing to move others toward commitment to Christ, and to display "glory in the church and in Christ Jesus throughout all generations, forever and ever" (Ephesians 3:21), then your infiltration is useless. So consider:

- Does your desire for change in your church stem from a deep desire to see other believers love God with all that they are and to live life to the fullest in Christ? Or do you just want lukewarm church people to wake up to their nastiness?

- Do you truly want to stand for Jesus at the risk of your appearance and reputation? Or do you just want to be a spiritual rebel?

- Do you really value what other believers have to say, and do you listen to them when they share their hearts with you? Or are you set on what you have to say, in the way you want to say it, to whomever you want to say it to?

- Do you try to live as though you are a part of an ideal church? Or do you infiltrate all the while thinking how horrible and screwed up and unchangeable your church is?

- Do you lay down your own wants and desires to help move others to Christ? Or do you do it to look like a super Christian for all the world to see?

Digging deep helps you examine your motives, which forces you to see yourself how God sees you. Infiltrators everywhere would do well to recite 1 Samuel 16:7 every time they cross under a steeple: "For the LORD sees not as man sees: man looks on the outward appearance, but the LORD looks on the heart."

> Humbly recognize that you have your own sin to deal with and that you won't succeed anywhere as a self-appointed leader.[5]
>
> Joshua Harris

Assess How Your Life Reflects the Commands of Jesus

> If you love me, you will keep my commandments (John 14:15).

Below are over thirty of Jesus's commands compiled into what I call *The Follower Manifesto*. Immersing yourself in it is a great way of assessing how your life reflects the call of Christ. But to truly immerse yourself requires something most don't do: reading out loud.

Saying something is much different than reading something. Whatever we say about ourselves falls under our own greater scrutiny because we wonder who's listening and whether or not they'd call us a liar.

That's why I don't just want you to read the following commands of Jesus like some laundry list. I want you to read them out loud. Slowly. Carefully. Because your conscience will let you know when you say something that's just not true about yourself.

> Developing the traits within a church does require honest self-evaluation—and that's not always easy.[6]
>
> Wayne Cordeiro

Letting *The Follower Manifesto* penetrate your soul is the first step to digging deep. Don't skip it. Find a room, close the door, and read the following out loud. Or read it as part of a group. As you do, listen for what the Holy Spirit, that voice deep inside you, whispers.

Especially if it says, "This isn't true about you."

The Follower Manifesto

- I am a follower of Jesus. I don't simply know about him. I *know* him. I have a relationship with him. He is my king and my savior, yet he is also my friend. I love him more than I can describe. I'm so alive when I'm in his presence. Sometimes I tear up in wonder, sometimes I laugh in astonishment. There isn't another person on the planet, not even a lifelong friend or family member, who stirs my soul like him. I'm not saying that just to sound Christian. I mean it.

- Jesus is the one I go to. He's the one I talk with. I may not hear his audible voice, but the clear nudges I get in my soul let me know that his Spirit is inside of me. I am in tune with him and refuse to ignore his promptings.

- Jesus is my identity. He is the reason that, no matter what life takes from me, I am still whole. Everything in my life—my passions, my possessions, my reputation, my popularity, my health, my dreams, my relationships— I've surrendered to him. He may change them. He may take them. He may leave them. They are his, not mine. I entrust him with everything that means anything to me.

- My life is about telling people about him. When I meet someone who doesn't know Jesus, my heart gets all caught up in how I might show the person his love and speak of his amazing truth.

- I'm always looking to serve others and invest in the lives of my friends, family, strangers—anyone whom God brings into my life. If I were to stand before Jesus today, I would smile at the few crowns I have to toss at his feet. Because I've given him everything.

- Because of Christ, I'm known as a loving person who listens well, encourages others, and refuses to bring up past wrongs in my relationships. I'm slow to anger and I make it a point to be there for people who are in a bind.

- I live with great security. I don't worry about things I can't control—and I know that I can't truly control *anything*.

- I don't bite back when other people mock me and my beliefs. Instead, I offer a gentle response, do good to the haters, pray for them, and even give to them without expecting anything back.

- I live a countercultural lifestyle that stands out. I may wear the same clothes and speak the same language as others, but when I am around people who don't know Jesus, they immediately know there's something different about me. More than once I've been asked, "What's up with you?"

- People who hang out with me don't have to search my words for exaggeration or embellishment. They know that my yes means yes and my no means no.

- I am peaceful when someone unjustly attacks my character or takes things that rightly belong to me. I'm known for turning the other cheek, knowing that God alone is just.

- Most of the things I do for the poor and needy go unnoticed. I tend to give money and help others in ways that do not draw attention.

- The money in my bank account and days on my calendar belong to God. When I see a need, I see an open invitation from God to give what he's freely given me—be it time or money. Doing so makes me happy.

- I'm known as someone who is wise, making sound decisions while also walking in whatever absurdity God calls me to. Strangers describe me as friendly, open, and easy to be around.

- When faced against some giant opposition, I pray and stay calm. I know the King of the world is with me and that he will supernaturally move me and give me words to say as he pleases.

- I live with a confidence that cannot be shaken, even when my life is threatened. Though people try to intimidate me, I stand strong knowing that my soul is secure forever.

- I talk about Jesus more than any other person. I tell others of the great things God has done for me and the mercy he's shown me. He's the person who comes up in conversations with people I'm getting to know. Without him, my identity is lost.

- I learn from Jesus every day. He's the first source I go to for insight and healing. If my time with him—praying, reading the Bible, pausing to think of him—were taken away, I don't know what I'd do.

- No matter what age, temperament, or differences, I look upon fellow believers as fellow heirs with Christ. I love them, I want to be there for them, and I want to serve them.

- I am the kind who forgives easily and often. I don't bring up past sins, either, knowing that doing so shows a lack of true forgiveness. I'm so indebted to Christ that I can't imagine not giving grace to others.

- Other believers know me more for what I do than what I do not do. They see the justice, mercy, and faithfulness I pursue in my day-to-day life. They know that my spirituality doesn't stand on a bunch of *do nots* in hopes that I'm good enough for God.

- Believers know that I look forward to God's return. They're sometimes taken aback at how real the return of Christ is to me because they just haven't paid much attention to it.

> Regrettably, it has become acceptable to sit in church week after week and do nothing but call yourself a follower of Christ.[7]
>
> Ed Stetzer

- I am known for telling others about Jesus and teaching them about him, both in word and deed. Doing this is more valuable to me than anything else in the world.

- I pray early and often throughout the day, asking grand things of God—yet always in submission to his will. I expect the unexpected, accept the unacceptable, and thank God for protecting me from temptation.

- I refuse to make bets with God or try to submit him to my little tests. Instead, I pray constantly for what he puts on my heart and I submit what I want to what *he* wants.

- I am always looking out for the needs of others, whether material or emotional. I ask God to reveal what I should do as I try to put myself into the hearts and minds of others and properly gauge how to bless them.

- I press onward in my walk with Jesus through the good and the bad, never looking back for what might have been had I never started the journey. The joy I have as a child of God is too overwhelming to ever consider anything else this world has to offer.

- I am the kind of person who stops to help those who are in need—alongside the road, at the grocery store, anywhere—even those who'd never consider doing the same for me.

- When it comes to money, possessions, and strict adherence to the letter of God's law, I check my heart constantly to see if there is any greed or hypocrisy in me.

- I humbly and sincerely tell my fellow believers when I've been hurt by them, knowing that honesty helps strengthen the relationship.

- When God has done great things through me, I humbly thank Jesus for letting me be a part of such an awesome work for the Kingdom. I never pat myself on the back, as though I deserve something for the work I'm supposed to do.

- Communion is a regular part of my life. I take it seriously because I do it in remembrance of what my God and king has done for me.

> In the end, God will not hold us accountable for what we have done. He will hold us accountable for how much we've done of what He asked us to do! [8]
>
> Wayne Cordeiro

By now, the Spirit of God has started a dialogue with you. He's whispered in your ear and perhaps nudged you in areas where you've grown numb to his Word. This is a good thing, even if it hurts.

The whole point of digging deep isn't

to weigh yourself down with guilt. It's to free yourself from it by con-fessing your imperfections to God, who unfailingly takes the weight off your shoulders and renews your spirit.

That said, guilt is not entirely bad. If your heart doesn't burn at your lack of devotion for Christ, then it will not burn the way it must to help your brothers' and sisters' devotion either.

Sometimes it's a very good thing to have a broken heart.

Allow Your Heart to Break Where It Needs Breaking

> For you will not delight in sacrifice, or I would give it; you will not be pleased with a burnt offering. The sacrifices of God are a broken spirit; a broken and contrite heart, O God, you will not despise (Psalm 51:16-17).

The second step to digging deep is to let yourself break.

We are sons and daughters of God and have instant access to him no matter where we are or what we're doing. But there's a great deal to be said of brokenness when it comes to approaching him about our lack of devotion to his Son.

> If you think you are basically a great person, and that anytime your conscience stirs it is simply some imbalance in your self-esteem, some feeling to be ignored or suppressed, then you are not following Christ.[9]
>
> Mark Dever

David didn't shrug off his sin and talk with God as though it were just another day after his sin with Bathsheba. He wept. He begged. His broken heart was his sacrifice. This is repentance, and it pleases God.

Infiltrators must break before we can ever help the church mend.

No one can really teach someone else how to break. It must come from your own heart in your own way. But there are still things that help the pro-cess. For me, it's the Peter Effect.

The Peter Effect is a visual process I use to engage with the injustice I commit every time I sin against Christ.

The Peter Effect: Remember, Visualize, Embrace

Remember

Peter was known as "the Rock." He was all-in for Jesus, so committed that his passion often got him into trouble. In studying Peter's early days as a believer, you get the sense that he wanted to be the first to do everything Jesus did and the first to follow him everywhere he went.

The first step of the Peter Effect is to remember who you are: a child of God who has given your life to Jesus. If you lose sight of this fact, then your breaking won't be healthy. Satan's forces will sneak in and tell you that you're a fraud whose sins are too great to ever be useful or forgiven. Don't listen. Remember whose child you are, and that it's a good thing to hurt when you've hurt your Father.

Visualize

Peter wasn't perfect. He committed the horrible sin of denying that he even knew Jesus—three times. I can't imagine what he felt the moment the rooster crowed. His breath must've left him in a quiet gasp. He probably put a fist to his mouth, trembling wildly. Everything that Jesus had told him would happen had happened. In that moment, he must have been breaking harder than most could ever fathom.

The second step of the Peter Effect is to visualize yourself, along with your various denials of Christ that the Spirit has made clear, in Peter's place. Your denial of Christ may look different from his, but it's still denial—a refusal to follow Jesus.

Not everyone is visually bent, but when I see my lack of devotion in a context as dark and heartbreaking as Peter's experience, I break. I see Jesus carrying his cross through the screaming, berating crowd in which I stand, and I break. Perhaps it will help you break as well.

Embrace

God didn't leave Peter in blackness. After Jesus had risen from the grave, conquering all sin and death, he sat with Peter and the other disciples for breakfast and asked Peter, "Do you truly love me?"

Peter answered, "Yes, Lord; you know that I love you."

"Feed my lambs," Jesus responded.

As Peter wondered about their short exchange, Jesus asked a second time, "Do you truly love me?"

Peter answered the same way.

"Take care of my sheep," Jesus responded.

Peter started feeling the same churn in his stomach he felt when he denied Christ. How he wished he could take everything back.

Jesus said a third time, "Do you love me?"

Peter, probably feeling sick now, responded, "Lord, you know all things; you know that I love you."

"Feed my sheep," Jesus replied.

The third step of the Peter Effect is to embrace total, passionate commitment to Christ. As far as we know, Jesus didn't go above and beyond in comforting Peter after his denials. Instead, he pushed Peter emotionally to embrace absolute devotion to him. He pushed Peter to do what he needed most. What we *all* need most.

Total commitment.

Devoting ourselves to Christ is to choose our greatest good. It's the best decision we can ever make, exchanging this world's emptiness for life-giving hope and peace. Jesus is not quick to help us choose anything less.

> There are many other important issues related to maturing in Christ, but an honest examination of our emotions and feelings is central to becoming more like Jesus. This inward look is not to encourage a self-absorbed introspection that feeds narcissism. The ultimate purpose is to allow the gospel to transform all of you.[10]
>
> Peter Scazzero

Pray for Restoration

Repent therefore, and turn back, that your sins may be blotted out, that times of refreshing may come from the presence of the Lord, and that he may send the Christ appointed for you, Jesus (Acts 3:19-20).

Too often I approach my lack of devotion flippantly. *Ah, what the heck—God forgives,* I think. *His grace has covered everything. Why let guilt rule me now? To think I can whip myself into his good graces is just another sin anyway.*

I don't try to think these things, but sometimes I do. I confuse brokenness before God with unrighteous self-lashing. I miss the beauty and blessing of digging deep: restoration.

Honestly assessing your devotion to Jesus means little without allowing your heart to break, and allowing your heart to break means little without restoration. This is why digging deep crescendos into a prayer of repentance and restoration, which Psalm 51 captures perfectly in three parts:

- Expressing sincere regret over your lack of devotion
- Yearning for a renewed spirit and closeness with God
- Overflowing with a desire to serve and worship him

David, the writer of the psalm, committed adultery and then tried to cover it up with murder. But are our sins any less? God says haughty eyes and those who stir up disunity among brothers and sisters are an abomination to him (Proverbs 6:16-19). And from what I've observed, these two sins are the greatest downfalls of the Frustrated and the Sieged. I know they were for me.

Close this chapter by immersing your lack of devotion to Jesus—no matter how much or how little—into these portions of Psalm 51. Read them and lose yourself for a while in the questions that follow.

Express

> Have mercy on me, O God, according to your steadfast love; according to your abundant mercy blot out my transgressions. Wash me thoroughly from my iniquity and cleanse me from my sin! For I know my transgressions, and my sin is ever before me. Against you, you only, have I sinned and done what is evil in your sight; so that you may be justified in your words and blameless in your judgment (Psalm 51:1-4).

Where is your devotion lacking to Jesus? What must you express sincere regret over? Don't hold back. Get past whatever Christian rhetoric and boundaries are tying you up and speak truthfully with God.

Yearn

> Create in me a clean heart, O God, and renew a right spirit within me. Cast me not away from your presence, and take not your Holy Spirit from me. Restore to me the joy of your salvation, and uphold me with a willing spirit (Psalm 51:10-12).

Do you yearn for closeness with your Savior? Do you sincerely want to turn away from the habits and sins that are grieving the Holy Spirit inside you? Don't just settle for honesty with God about your lack of devotion. Grab his ankles and cry out for him to lift you up to true, passionate commitment.

Overflow

> Then I will teach transgressors your ways, and sinners will return to you. Deliver me from bloodguiltiness, O God, O God of my salvation, and my tongue will sing aloud of your righteousness. O Lord, open my lips, and my mouth will declare your praise (Psalm 51:13-15).

Too often we get into the habit of sighing relief after we've been forgiven of a nasty sin. David shows us that we should instead overflow with a desire to do the things that are most important to God.

In what ways do you now, after confessing your wrongs and asking for forgiveness, long to serve Jesus? In what ways might you worship him all the more? Don't just be happy that your debt is paid in full. Get excited about giving your life to the one who gave his life for you.

What Now?

Watch this chapter's video at www.calledtostay.com.

Dowload a copy of "The Follower Manifesto" at www.calledtostay .com.

"Digging deep helps me..." — Post this as your Facebook status and I'll join the conversation (just remember to tag me).

What's Next

Brokenness and a desire to pour yourself into your relationship with Jesus makes soft clay of your soul—but it doesn't have the power to transform you. You need something far more powerful for that.

The Holy Spirit.

If we want to powerfully infiltrate the body of Christ, we must get in touch with the Spirit of God inside us. Without the living, pulsing presence of God in our souls, we are powerless to help others commit their lives to Jesus.

CHAPTER 5

Who You Must Embrace

Unleash God's Power Inside You

> My speech and my message were not in plausible words of wisdom, but in demonstration of the Spirit and of power, so that your faith might not rest in the wisdom of men but in the power of God (1 Corinthians 2:4-5).

You know it when you see it.

Whether they're world leaders, random folks at a coffee shop, or superstar athletes, certain people have a presence about them. They *fascinate* us.

Infiltrators are commanded to add spiritual flavor to the world (Matthew 5:13). We're commanded to be captivating (Matthew 5:14-16). Not in a look-at-us sort of way, but in a look-at-God sort of way. The problem is that most of us are not. We've hidden the power of God deep inside us.

We've locked up the Holy Spirit.

This is the Spirit Jesus said was more important to us than his physical presence. The Spirit who mysteriously intercedes for us even while we're unaware. The Spirit whose great power is available to us every day of our lives. The Spirit we, as author Francis Chan puts it, tragically neglect.

The Holy Spirit is confirmation that Jesus lives in us (Acts 2:38). He is the reason we proclaim, "Jesus is in my heart." He is who makes us loving, controlled, and even *powerful* (2 Timothy 1:7). He comforts us, reveals truth to us, convicts us, and prompts us to action (John 14:25-27). He stirs love, joy, peace, patience, kindness, goodness, faithfulness, gentleness, and self-control in us (Galatians 5:22-23). The Spirit isn't just a part of theology. He's central to our identity as followers of Christ.

Or at least he should be.

Let me ask: If some witch cast a spell on you today, somehow making the Spirit dwell elsewhere for a week, would you notice a change in your life? If we are ever to stir the body of Christ to passionately commit to Jesus, we must embrace the Spirit of God, who transforms our lives from mere words and actions into a demonstration of his power.

> Rarely (if ever) do we consider whether our actions or lifestyle are grievous to the Spirit of the living God.[1]
>
> Francis Chan

> If you then, who are evil, know how to give good gifts to your children, how much more will the heavenly Father give the Holy Spirit to those who ask him! (Luke 11:13).

In Acts 1, while eating one of his final meals with his disciples before ascending into heaven, Jesus told his good friends to *wait*.

They were not ready to show and tell the amazing news of Christ. It didn't matter that they'd spent three years with him. They lacked something so significant that Jesus told them to wait.

For what?

"For the gift my Father promised, which you have heard me speak about…the Holy Spirit" (Acts 1:4-5 NIV).

> The truth is, we can be in relationship with God and active in helping others for years without really understanding His ways or allowing Him to work through us in supernatural ways.[2]
>
> Bruce Wilkinson

Jesus told his disciples that through the Spirit they'd receive power *and then* be his messengers to the ends of the earth. He made them wait because no Spirit meant no power to deliver the message.

This chapter helps you deliver the message with power by unleashing the might of God's Spirit that's been inside you since you gave your life to Christ.

If you know Jesus, the Spirit already dwells in you and cannot be added to your life. But you can ask God for a more intimate connection with his Spirit (Luke 11:13). You can make room for the Spirit in your life (1 Corinthians 3:16-18). You can stand ready and alert for the Spirit's next move in bringing glory to God (1 Peter 1:13).

The Lord's eyes are roaming the earth for believers sold out to following and worshipping his Son. And the Spirit empowers us to follow and worship Jesus humbly and fearlessly.

Why You Must Be Superhuman

> And we all, with unveiled face, beholding the glory of the Lord, are being transformed into the same image from one degree of glory to another. For this comes from the Lord who is the Spirit (2 Corinthians 3:18).

You're not alone if you have reservations about God's Holy Spirit.

Up until my late teens, I thought of the Spirit as an "it" that helped me understand the Bible and be a good Christian. That's it. When I started learning more about the Spirit's role in a believer's life, I thought it was kind of weird and out there. *I haven't heard this before*, I'd think.

The fact that the Spirit cannot be understood is the core problem. We fear that which we don't understand, and we stay away from that which we fear.

But God doesn't want us going through life fearful. He wants us living in power and love and self-control. He wants us going through life knowing that he's truly in our hearts, ready to help us follow Jesus and encourage others to do the same. He promises to comfort us, help us, intercede for us, empower our gifts, and give us wisdom and deep conviction.

And he comes through in his promises.

God drew me into intimacy with his Spirit through events in my life that radically changed my understanding of God and devotion to Jesus.

He showed me that he would speak for me when I didn't know what to say. He showed me that his Spirit would only and always direct me to do his will—even if it seemed crazy. And he showed me that his power, which is far beyond comprehension, was available to me always. It's not that any of these are novel concepts. It's that God showed me that I wasn't created just to *know* these things. I was created to experience them in real life. All the time.

> I want people to look at my life and know that I couldn't be doing this by my own power. I want to live in such a way that I am desperate for Him to come through…I don't believe God wants me (or any of His children) to live in a way that makes sense.[3]
>
> Francis Chan

There is incredible power living inside every Infiltrator. But not every Infiltrator lives powerfully.

This must change if you want to give Jesus Christ and his bride all that you are and all that you are meant to be.

When You Don't Have Words

The first time I experienced the Holy Spirit was in a college classroom when I was seventeen. Before that, I completely squelched the Spirit. I thought of him as some abstract part of God that did all of the behind-the-scenes work of my soul that I never needed to pay attention to.

But that started to change in the classroom.

Scared out of my mind and unconfident in my knowledge of Scripture, I walked to the front of the class to talk about the book of Job. I was preparing myself to get shredded and, in desperation, cried out to God: *Help. I can't do this.*

> Irresistible churches are champions at leading people closer to God, being conduits for the Holy Spirit to change lives for the better and impact society for good.[4]
>
> Wayne Cordeiro

I didn't think much of that prayer until after it was all over.

Throughout my presentation, classmates questioned me and spewed about Job being a frivolous story about two divine beings playing games. But out of nowhere, I calmly responded to their questions with a kind of power and authority I didn't know I had. Words came to me that I hadn't prepared. Rational, biblical defense diffused the sense of mockery created in the classroom. Verses and truths presented themselves as though served on a platter to my tongue.

At some point while talking I realized that something supernatural was going on. I felt as though God had stuck a tube into my brain and was feeding me everything I needed.

After my presentation, I walked to my car, plopped inside, and prayed in tears. *You did that, didn't you?*

The God of the universe somehow heard my cry and met me in a junior college classroom. He swooped in and gave me a glimpse of the Holy Spirit's power inside me. The whole experience was like God leaning close to my ear and whispering, "When you don't have the words, my Spirit will."

You Will Never Do Wrong

Years later, I felt God nudging me to quit my job as a sports journalist. I'd wanted to change careers before, so that wasn't new. The big difference was that, this time, it wasn't me wanting to quit. It was something, or Someone, else.

> Have you ever come to a point in your life where you've had to make a choice between everything visible... and something invisible, something inaudible, something known only to you that you can't possibly defend *but that you know in your heart is true?* [5]
>
> Bruce Wilkinson

And that felt weird.

For three months, I wrestled with making sense of it. My wife and I talked about the situation openly. It was too dangerous to quit my job, I'd say. The money would run out. Why would God want me to do this? Was it really from him?

The last thing I wanted to do was quit my job because "God told me to" when he really hadn't. But how could I know for sure? So just like I did in that college classroom, I prayed: *Please make it clear what you want me to do.*

For two months after that, I got a strong spiritual vibe that I would be done with journalism. But it wasn't just strong. It was precise. I kept telling my wife: "I think God is going to do something in mid-March."

By February, two months later, nothing had changed—until I received a phone call while covering a high school basketball game. The guy on the other line was a friend I hadn't spoken with in over a year. "Hey!" he said. "You got a minute? I think I've got something you might be interested in."

My friend told me that he was stepping away from a job that he thought I might want to check out—one that would pay the bills and give me flexibility to write words that were more meaningful than 500-word articles.

> God is still real and moving, but at some point we have to respond and act because of what He's done. Like yeast and flour are both necessary to bread, both God's actions and our response-action are necessary in this relationship with God.[6]
>
> Francis Chan

"Wow, that sounds incredible," I said. "When does it open up?"

"Mid-March," he responded.

Words, let alone breath, struggled to journey from my lungs to my mouth. Was God really doing this? Was he making it that clear?

To make a long story short, the next thing God put on my heart was for me to quit my journalism job before I heard whether or not I was hired for the new job. It was illogical. It was stupid. It freaked me out.

But it was from God, and I knew it.

"I don't want to do this," I remember telling my wife. "But I *know* I'd be sinning if I didn't. And that tells me this is from him. It's a James 4:17 thing."

> Whoever knows the right thing to do and fails to do it, for him it is sin (James 4:17).

I quit my job the next day, and people thought I was nuts. *I* kind of thought I was nuts. But I felt at peace.

A few days later I got the job, signed with a literary agent (after two years of trying), and eventually signed a contract to write this book. All along, it was God saying, "Listen to my Spirit, and you will never do wrong."

Power Like You've Never Seen

Writing for God eventually led to speaking about him as well.

One day at a conference of about four hundred people, I needed to get on stage and give a short talk about who I was and what I was teaching. You'd think this would be easy. I loved Jesus with all of my heart, and I was going to be teaching about writing. But the moment I got to the stage steps to wait for the signal, my knees started shaking. Badly. I couldn't see it, but I'm sure my face reddened. I hoped no one was watching.

This wasn't the first time something like this had happened.

A year earlier at a writers retreat, I had to give a devotional in front of other writers—the leader of which was Jerry B. Jenkins, author of the bestselling Left Behind series. My legs shook crazily the entire time. And when I made eye contact with Jerry mid-devotion, his eyes were locked on my knees as if mesmerized by how they could shake on an unmoving body. I thought I'd die.

Just as I thought I'd die on stage.

But just before I was about to climb the steps, I prayed: *God, Holy Spirit, please calm me right now.* And in an instant—I mean *instant*—my body relaxed. I stood there dumbfounded for a moment, half expecting the shakes to come back with a vengeance. So I immediately said: *Thank you, Lord*, and got on stage. The shakes never returned, and I glorified Jesus from the stage with strength of voice and an easygoing demeanor.

> Miracles are never an end in themselves; they are always a means to point to and accomplish something greater.[7]
>
> Francis Chan

When I returned to my seat, I realized that I had, for the first time in my life, addressed the Holy Spirit directly in my prayers. That got me thinking. God didn't *need* me to address the Spirit. But the immediate response to my prayer was like God saying, "Be intimate with my Spirit, and I will show you power like you've never seen."

> It's the difference between your feeling good about what you've done to help others and others feeling astonished by what God has done for them through you.[8]
>
> Bruce Wilkinson

Embrace Superhumanity

If God had not explicitly taught me these things about his Spirit, I wouldn't be infiltrating today. It's simply impossible to move others toward Jesus if the Spirit is dormant in your own life.

No longer do I wonder if I'll have the right words to say in tough situations in the body of Christ—or anywhere. No longer do I wonder if God will show me what he wants me to do, even if it looks like certain disaster. No longer do I wonder if I truly have a connection to the supernatural power of God.

I do. I have a relationship with the Spirit of God. I talk with him. I listen for him. This closeness has led to a life of greater conviction, confidence, compassion, and love. I am fully alive in Christ. Or, to put it another way, I am superhuman.

That's the effect of the Holy Spirit in our lives.

Now is the time to embrace the power of God inside you. Now is the time to choose a lifestyle that fascinates others with the truth and love of Christ. Now is the time to become superhuman.

How to Keep Emotions from Running Amuck

My friend told me that while alone in his office one day, an intense feeling overwhelmed him to worship God. Right then and there. No questions asked. Just, *worship me*. It was a surreal experience for him.

> Once a leading is confirmed as aligned with Scripture, the specific leading of the Holy Spirit is discerned intuitively.[9]
>
> Wayne Cordeiro

Later, though, he confessed that he wasn't sure if he was just having an emotional experience or if it was truly the Spirit stirring him to worship. I understood where he was coming from. There are a ton of people in this world who claim they "received a word from the Lord" when clearly they didn't (like something that completely goes against Scripture). There are also a ton of people who say "it just felt right"—when really, "just feeling right" meant having sex with someone they shouldn't have.

Emotional experiences can run amuck.

But life without emotional experiences is already run amuck. Because without them, we completely ignore the Spirit of God.

Many of us fall into the trap of believing that God only speaks through Scripture. We don't embrace the fact that God also *confirms* through Scripture. This means that we do not need a verse to confirm, word for word, whatever the Spirit stirs inside us. We only need to confirm whether or not the stirring fits our biblical purpose, which is to glorify God and enjoy him forever.

The implication for Infiltrators is that we need to start confirming Spirit-led feelings through the simple calling of glorifying God and enjoying him.

- Have you ever felt compelled to invest love or encouragement in someone, but ignored it?

- Have you ever experienced a burning desire to get involved in a book study or ministry, but shaken it off?

- Have you ever felt compelled to give your money away, only to let the opportunity slip?

Might any of these nudges have brought glory to God? Might any of these have helped you enjoy him? What if these feelings were actual whispers from God to you through his Spirit?

It's easier to respond to a "Thou shalt" than it is to an emotion, but God speaks to us through both. Jesus says that the Spirit only speaks what God tells him to speak (John 16:13-15). So whether something is stated in Scripture or an emotion confirmed by Scripture, we can know it's good and true.

> Why do we sometimes feel that we need to debate this endlessly, running through every possible hypothetical situation and answering every theological question first? When will we simply respond to the truth we have heard and then work through our questions from there? [10]
>
> Francis Chan

If we are to be successful in stirring up a greater commitment to Jesus, we must stop ignoring nudges from the Spirit and start confirming them instead.

The Story of Jack

There once was a man named Jack. When Jack became a Christian, a mysterious ball appeared right in the middle of his house. At first he thought it was cool. The thing was like an oversized bowling ball and it glowed like the moon. Every once in a while, he was convinced it had a mind of its own because it would roll this way and that without any warning. Sometimes Jack would stay up at night, asking it to roll to the left or right or bounce. Every once in a while, it would. But most of the time, it was pretty unpredictable.

But having a big glowing ball in your living room made him self-conscious when others visited. So, after having explained the ball to numerous friends and family, he finally decided to clear out his living room closet and jam it in there. It took a lot of work because the ball was bigger than the doorway. But about one hundred hard pushes and a few cracks in the wall later, he had it in there and the door shut. He wasn't sure if he'd ever get the door open again. But that wasn't a problem, really.

The days following were bliss. Jack had so much more room! He bought a bigger TV, the newest and best gaming technology, extra couches, more lamps, a few tiki torches (just because they're cool), and even a futon he found online. It was awesome. He knew this because his friends told him so every time they came over.

What's even better is that they never mentioned the glowing ball again. It's like they didn't even remember it was there.

Months and years passed and Jack kept filling his living room with more stuff than he knew what to do with. Then one day, while experimenting with his indoor miniature golf course, he putted and accidentally wedged the ball underneath his closet door. As he shoved the clutter aside with the heel of his shoe, a tremendous light shone into his living room from under the door.

His ball.

Jack looked around, wondering if anyone was watching. He backed up and stared at the door, remembering what his living room used to look like, the conversations he used to have with friends and family, and the late nights he spent stupidly trying to tell the ball what to do. He really missed those days. Everything was so much less cluttered and…simple.

He studied the door. Would it be possible to get the ball out? He tried the handle. It didn't budge. Jack next pressed his foot against the door for leverage. He yanked as hard as he could. Nothing.

Frustrated and hot in the face, he pounded his fist against the door. Then kicked it. But the door still showed no sign of loosening. Jack slumped down with his back against the door, staring down at the light creeping out from underneath. He wanted to see the ball again so badly.

After an hour of sitting slumped, depressed, Jack got an idea. He spoke with ball, just like he had all those nights ago. "Would you please come out again?" he said.

Nothing happened, so he asked again. And again. But after ten minutes of asking, it dawned on him that maybe the ball didn't want to come out because it knew that even if it could fit through the door, there'd be no place for it anymore. The living room was a mess with all of his junk.

Without giving it any more thought, Jack opened his front door, grabbed his snow shovel from the garage, and started shoving out all of his junk in long, sweeping motions. The mountains of garbage rolled out of his front door and onto his lawn like a garage sale landslide.

He worked nonstop for hours, never registering that his neighbors were coming out of their houses, robes on, coffee cups in hand. The fact that he'd worked through the night didn't occur to him.

Finally, a friend grabbed Jack by his shoulders just as he was piling another load onto the lawn. Jack jolted to attention. "What?"

"Jack, it's me. You know, your friend? I came over as soon as I heard. What are you doing?"

"Getting rid of junk!" Jack said, smiling. He tried lunging back into the house but his friend stopped him.

"Why?" the friend said. "You're not moving, are you?"

"No, it's my ball."

His friend's tone flatlined. "Not the big glowing one."

"Yes!"

"Please, don't tell me you're trashing your great stuff just to put that stupid ball back in your living room."

"Yep!" This time, Jack ran back inside before his friend could stop him.

"You're making a mistake, Jack!" his friend called out.

But Jack wasn't paying attention. He was on a mission.

By that evening, Jack's living room was back to the way it once was. Simple, easy, and with plenty of room for his ball. He silently approached the door. The glow shining from below was much brighter now with the clutter removed.

"Would you please come out again?" Jack waited. But again, nothing. "Please, I won't ever put you in this closet again. Just come out."

Jack stood back from the door and stared at it intently. Not a sound, not a movement. His limbs ached from the long night of work. His eyelids wanted to close. Jack grabbed a chair and set it up in the middle of his living room, facing the door. He sat and watched, occasionally spraying his face with water to keep him awake. A few times he leaned on his hand and started drifting. But he promptly jolted back up, keeping his eyes on the door. He needed to be ready. If he so much as saw an inch of movement or extra glimmer of—

The ball moved. It was slight, but the ball moved in the closet. "Yes, here we go." Jack got up and pressed his ear to the door. The ball's movement intensified. Its glow turned white hot under the door and through all of the door's cracks. The door handle started shaking. The floor started shaking. The entire house started shaking.

The ball wanted out and it was trying to get out. Now was the time. Jack grabbed the handle with both hands in spite of the heat, gritted his teeth, and yanked as hard as he could.

He fell backward into his living room as something burst over his head. Whatever it was flew like ginormous shrapnel through his living room window and onto his front lawn with all of his other junk.

Light that seemed as bright as the surface of the sun shone all around Jack. He wiped debris off his face and sat upright, straining to see through the brightness. But before he could see a thing, he smiled.

Because he heard the distinct sound of the large glowing ball leaving the closet and rolling his way. Jack flopped his head back and laughed.

He stood and looked at the ball as its light began to recede to the point he could see. Outside his broken living room window stood his friends, neighbors, friends of friends, neighbors of neighbors, and a bunch of other people he'd never seen. They all looked at him as though he were from another planet.

He smiled and turned to the ball. "So great to have you back."

3 Steps to Intimacy

Jack's glowing ball is like the Holy Spirit. When we gave our lives to Christ, we became new creations and God breathed his Spirit into us. From that moment on, we were fundamentally different. Our countenance was changed forever.

But just like Jack, many of us put the Spirit in a closet and fill our lives with junk—maybe without even realizing it. We hide the very presence that distinguishes us "from all the other people on the face of the earth" (Exodus 33:16). We stuff down the power that astonishes people and makes them recognize that we are close to Jesus.

How do we go about releasing the glowing ball back into the center of our lives? There are only three things I know to do:

- Ask God
- Make room
- Stand ready

Ask God

> Ask, and it will be given to you; seek, and you will find; knock, and it will be opened to you. For everyone who asks receives, and the one who seeks finds, and to the one who knocks it will be opened (Matthew 7:7-8).

When Jack got it into his head that he needed to get his glowing ball back, he got hot in the face trying to get it out. But the closet door wouldn't budge. If it were going to come out, it would have to do it through its own power. So as ridiculous as it may have seemed to him, Jack asked the ball to do just that.

We need to do the same. We need to ask God to move his Spirit into the center of our lives, just as Paul asked God that we'd become more aware of the hope and power that's available to us and use it to glorify Jesus.

Not through trite prayer. But through fervent prayer. And not for our own personal gain or to advance our own agenda. But to serve others and reflect Christ in a way that shouts of God's great glory to the people around us.

> A sure sign of the Holy Spirit's working is that Christ is magnified, not people.[11]
>
> Francis Chan

If your desire for intimacy with the Spirit is anything less than to love more, serve more, and worship more, then you're asking in vain.

Make Room

> Do you not know that you are God's temple and that God's Spirit dwells in you?...God's temple is holy, and you are that temple (1 Corinthians 3:16-17).

Nothing happened after Jack initially asked the glowing ball to come out. So what did he do? He looked around at all the junk in his living room and started clearing it out. He made an honest assessment about his messy house and decided that, if he were the ball, he'd be much more likely to come out if there were actually room. So he made room.

We must do the same.

To make room for the Holy Spirit in our lives, we need less of ourselves. Pride is the ultimate Spirit-killer. Humility, though, is the ultimate Spirit-igniter. It's what strips us of perceived earthly power and makes room for God to clothe us in spiritual power. It's the key to making room for the Spirit.

But humility is just a word. It's a truth on a page that has no power to change our lives unless we actively pursue it. We need traction, something to go on. We'll look at this more in the next chapter, which is dedicated entirely to the secret of humility and making room.

Stand Ready

> Therefore, preparing your minds for action, and being sober-minded, set your hope fully on the grace that will be brought to you at the revelation of Jesus Christ (1 Peter 1:13).

Jack asked and nothing happened. He made room and nothing happened. So he simply stood ready.

If we are ever to be intimate with God's Spirit, we need to remain constantly alert to what he might be up to. This means paying attention when we feel something out of the ordinary. Or sense something unusual in our circumstances. Or just know intuitively that God is stirring inside us.

When we stand ready, God has a way of inviting us to play a role in his glorious plans—including his plans for the church. Things start to happen. God shows us that his Spirit speaks for us. He reveals his will to us and nudges us toward it. And he empowers us supernaturally when we simply cannot do something ourselves.

Like changing the church.

The key is to refuse cynicism. So when you become more loving, controlled, and powerful, don't just *think* that it might be from the Spirit of God. Know it.

When you're comforted or begin to understand hard truths of Scripture, know it's the Spirit. When you believe you've been invisibly helped, give praise to God through his Spirit. When you do or say something powerfully awesome for the glory of God, thank God through his Spirit. And when emotion lifts you into euphoria because of the love and hope you have in Christ, praise the work of the Spirit.

> As you look around at your brothers and sisters, do you think to yourself, "I love these people so much. I pray God empowers me in some way to encourage these people toward a deeper walk with Him"? [12]
>
> Francis Chan

Don't get that glazed feeling when God is at work. Just confirm it through Scripture. Ask whether it might glorify God or help you enjoy him.

And stand ready.

Be a Living Stone

> You yourselves like living stones are being built up as a spiritual house, to be a holy priesthood, to offer spiritual sacrifices acceptable to God through Jesus Christ (1 Peter 2:5).

More than once I've heard someone say, "I'm not sure I really understand the Holy Spirit."

Me either. No one ever will. All we can do is ask. Make room. And stand ready. When we do these things, we are truly *living* stones, ready and waiting for God to use us to build his church.

> We are the city on the hill. We are Times Square in the darkness. We are the church of the living God. Now live like it.[13]
>
> Ed Stetzer

The Holy Spirit isn't a switch that can be flicked on in our lives. But you might be surprised at how quickly God moves in those who desire to be intimate with his Spirit, live like his Son, do his work, and build his church.

What Now?

Watch this chapter's video at www.calledtostay.com.

Get the download of "3 Steps to Intimacy" here: www.calledtostay.com.

"The Holy Spirit empowered me to..." — Post this as your Facebook status and I'll join the conversation (just remember to tag me).

What's Next

How exactly do you make room for the Holy Spirit in your life? There's one word that answers this question perfectly: *childlikeness*. Even if you finish this book and decide that infiltrating isn't God's call for you, childlikeness is. It's what makes you see things as they truly are. It allows you to make incredibly difficult decisions with peace. And most importantly, it unleashes the viral-like presence that helps liberate others from mediocrity and push them to full-on commitment to Jesus.

CHAPTER 6

What Comes Next

How to Unsettle Other Believers

One of the most important aspects of infiltration looks spiritually stupid.

Back in my teens, I went to a camp called Christian Youth In Action. While I was there, I lost my bag of favorite gel pens. (I admit, I'm kind of laughing at myself right now. How many guys take a bag of gel pens to camp?) A friend who was several years younger than me approached me about them. "Have you found your pens yet?" he said.

"No. I'm pretty sure they're a goner."

"Have you prayed about it?"

Now, fast-forward a few years to a comfy rental car on the island of Hawaii, Hawaii. A friendly lady my wife and I had met at a writing conference was taking us out to a very nice restaurant overlooking the ocean. And while circling the place's tiny parking lot, she started praying. "Well Jesus, here we are. Where do you think we should park?" She circled around the cramped lot a few times, asking Jesus for a parking space.

Just as we turned to circle once more, parking lights lit up in one of closest spaces to the entrance. "Thank you, Jesus!" she said.

These are just two instances that stand out when I think of childlikeness.

The adult in us might look at my friends and think, "Ha! Praying

> A subtle message has filtered into our churches that to be human, to be emotional, is somehow sinful—or at least less than spiritual.[1]
>
> Peter Scazzero

for pens and parking places! How immature can you be?" What the adult in us fails to realize is that true maturity is the person humble enough to entrust to God not only life's bigger issues, but its smaller ones too.

In infrequent doses, people snicker at childlikeness. But when confronted with it on a consistent basis, a beautiful unsettling starts to stir. It discomforts those unwilling to fully humble themselves or trust God.

What is so different about that believer? a believer wonders. *How can they be so immature but seem so close to God?* Thoughts like these are the beginning of liberation for those in the church who are going through the motions or trapped in pharisaical snares. They're the result of childlikeness and the celebration of infiltration.

They mean that people can see you walk with Jesus.

They mean the presence of God distinguishes you from others.

They mean you're pointing people toward a greater commitment.

Believers do not change their commitment level to Jesus because of another believer who's just like them. They change because the other believer is radically different—someone who radiates freedom and love.

...like children do.

But many of us don't possess the awe and wonder of a child. We let our fear of others eradicate the everyday reality of our sonship of God. We conform to what the world—and, in many cases, our own brothers and sisters—want us to be: normal.

This robs us of influence in our churches.

It's true that God wants us to grow in our knowledge and obedience of him, but he never wants us to stop living with the humility, trust, and the absolute abandonment of a child. We see this throughout Scripture.

God's eyes are on the childlike, guiding them, teaching them, and smiling at them (Isaiah 66:2, Psalm 25:9, Luke 14:11, Romans 12:16, James 4:6). He fights for them, carries them, and shows them where to go and what to do (Deuteronomy 1:30-33). It's as if they have an impenetrable strength and shield, and are always being helped (Psalm 28:7).

The childlike are never fearful of bad news (Psalm 112:7). They never lean on their own understanding (Proverbs 3:5). They prosper in good times and bad (Proverbs 28:25). The countenance of the childlike shines like the dawn, and their work on earth like the noonday sun (Psalm 37:5-6). They trust God even when they're afraid, and they conquer their fear with trust (Psalm 52:8, 56:4). God never forsakes them, nor does he put them to shame (Psalm 9:10, 25:3).

The childlike have a perfect peace about them (Isaiah 26:3). A song of praise to God is always on their mouth (Psalm 40:3). Every day, they confidently and proudly look up and say, "You are my God" (Psalm 31:14).

I'm the kind of person who likes to sing to God and express myself before him. When I'm alone and praying, I often kneel or completely prostrate myself before him. I readily welcome tears whenever they come upon me. I like showing God my love through abandoned emotion and trust.

> Nothing brings glory down in church as quickly and as powerfully as when God's people unashamedly adore God's great Son, Jesus Christ.[2]
> James MacDonald

But can you imagine acting this way in a busy parking lot, or supermarket, or movie theater? Can you imagine doing these things in a coffee shop, or airport, or family gathering? It would be pretty weird. Pretty awkward. People would probably think you'd lost it. Yet you'd have their attention. You'd have a captive audience.

This is what childlikeness does in the body of Christ.

Why You Must Become Childlike

Children are fun. Children are loving. They hold the key to more hearts than any other on the face of earth. We take videos and snap pictures, trying to remember every moment. It's a special time that goes away. We don't try to capture memories in our twenties or thirties near as much as we try to capture the memories of childhood. Humans are not meant to stay childlike.

Unless you're a follower of Jesus.

Childlikeness Frees Us from Conformity

> And calling to him a child, he put him in the midst of them and said, "Truly, I say to you, unless you turn and become like children, you will never enter the kingdom of heaven" (Matthew 18:2-3).

The humility and trust of childlikeness separate us from the concept of control and point others to the reality that the more control we give to God, the more freedom he gives to us.

Conformity, on the other hand, makes us slaves to purposelessness. It fools us into thinking that what we *don't do* is our salt and light. Such as not watching R-rated movies, not drinking, or not staying up past 2 a.m. (though there's certainly nothing wrong with these standards).

> As a church, we tend to do this to people who are passionate and bold. We mellow them out. Institutionalize them. Deaden them to the work that the Spirit is doing in them...We read of the early church doing just the opposite.[3]
>
> Francis Chan

Instead of adhering to spoken or unspoken *do nots*, childlikeness unleashes you to light up the world with what you *do*.

Like smiling. Like asking genuine questions of everyone you come across because you're interested in them as human beings. Or praying over people no matter where you are or who is around. Or singing to God while on a walk. Or gushing over things most people don't, such as the sky, or the trees, or the groceries you just bought with the money God provided. Or speaking about Jesus as though he were really alive, really with you, and really changing your life every moment of every day.

This is childlikeness, and Infiltrators must aspire to it.

Childlikeness Frees Us from Pride

> Clothe yourselves, all of you, with humility toward one another, for "God opposes the proud but gives grace to the humble" (1 Peter 5:5).

Childlikeness frees us from pride by humbling us.

Where adults nuance things to make them look better, children are *real*. They haven't adapted to everything we adults would consider social norms. When my little brother-in-law was four or five, he shouted to his mom in a crowded Costco parking lot, "Hey Mom! Dad just tooted three times!" I'm not suggesting losing all your inhibitions, but we can learn from this child's realness.

How many times have you thought to yourself: *I don't want someone at church to know this about me. Or think this about me. Or misunderstand me.*

We want our fellow believers to think we're strong Christians. So we avoid saying and doing things that might show weakness or come off as un-Christian. This isn't childlike. This is putting up a front out of fear.

God wants us to clean the inside of our cup, not the outside. So, like a child, humbly choose to care more about what God thinks of you than what others think of you.

> Whoever exalts himself will be humbled, and whoever humbles himself will be exalted (Matthew 23:12).

Have you ever listened to a child apologize? It can be hilarious. Instead of just saying, "Sorry," some kids retell their entire drama. It doesn't come out, "I'm sorry for hurting you." It comes out, "I'm sorry for throwing the Lincoln Logs at your face and putting my Hot Wheels in your ear and sitting on your head."

Saying "sorry" is easy. Saying what you're sorry for is hard. But when you tell others exactly how you've sinned against them, you are humble and childlike.

> Confess your sins to one another and pray for one another, that you may be healed (James 5:16).

Children aren't ashamed of things they don't know or understand. When adults don't know something—like a fact about the world, or their government, or how to say "aluminum," as is my case—we avoid it and hope it's never brought up. Too embarrassing.

Children, on the other hand, ask question after question in light of their lack of knowing. "Why? Why? Why?" is their drumbeat.

Think about this in terms of Scripture. Most of us think we know the right things about the Bible and believe the right things. Few of us would ever think that our understanding is lacking, especially in our spiritual lives. If we did, we'd do something about it.

Becoming childlike puts an end to getting defensive whenever a brother or sister tries to correct you spiritually. It ends your desire to simply not be wrong and instead makes you correctable and hungry for the truth.

> Poverty and disgrace come to him who ignores instruction,
> but whoever heeds reproof is honored (Proverbs 13:18).

Bringing a child to pretty much any athletic event, no matter how insignificant—such as church softball or any recreational league—is awesome if you're playing. Because they look at you as though you're a rockstar.

> It is, first of all, the freedom of the other person, of which we spoke earlier, that is a burden to the Christian.[4]
>
> Dietrich Bonhoeffer

After every ballgame my little nephew watches, he runs up to me immediately after the game (or during) and starts asking me all sorts of questions about what I'm doing. He's like a little reporter, only interested in the star athlete. The thing is, I'm no star athlete! He just thinks I am.

Becoming childlike helps you put the spotlight on others. Instead of being wrapped up in your job and your goals and your passions, you start asking others about their jobs and goals and passions.

> Do nothing from selfish ambition or conceit, but in humility count others more significant than yourselves (Philippians 2:3).

The Story of Lena

There once was a child named Lena, and she loved her father tremendously. She followed him everywhere he went. She listened for his car to pull into the driveway. She loved him and told everyone about him—even though no one really wanted to hear it.

See, her dad had this thing about him that people just couldn't get past: He never showed himself. He'd do his work in secret, like a ghost. So even though Lena told people about the great work he was doing, they were skeptical of whether or not her father was real.

One day, Trix, who lived down the street a ways, approached her with an idea: "Look, Lena, you talk about your dad all the time, but none of us have ever seen him. I'm worried about you. The neighbors are worried about you. Some even think that someone is slipping you poison that makes you see things. Why don't you come over to my house for a while, pick weeds for me, eat what my family eats, and then see whether or not your father is real."

Lena agreed and went to work picking weeds. Every so often, Trix would bring her food and chat a few minutes. But the day just never seemed to end.

Finally, Trix approached her again with another meal. "Look who's back!" he said. But there was something different about him. He'd gotten shorter! Or had she gotten taller? Lena looked down, seeing someone different from herself. She was taller. Older. Like an adult.

"You okay?" Trix said.

"What's going on?" She rubbed her arms.

But Trix seemed confused. "What do you mean? You're just picking weeds."

"I'm done, Mr. Trix. I'm going back to be with my father."

"What father?" he said.

Lena dropped her tools and ran back home. When she made it back, her house was gone. Everything was gone. What was going on? Her breathing quickened. Was she going crazy?

Then a thought hit her. One last place to look.

She took off down the trail behind where the house used to be. At the end was the bench where she used to sit on her father's lap, feet dangling over the side in anticipation of a sunrise. Lena pulled up, breathless. The bench was gone. She crumpled into a ball on the ground. And there she cried all night, wondering if her father had ever been real.

The next morning, as the sun rose, all she could think about was her father and her many talks with him in this exact spot. Then she did something that felt a little foolish. She mimicked how she used to sit on the bench, propping her head against her arm, pretending it was daddy.

As she looked at the rising orange ball, she talked as if he were there with her. Sometimes in midsentence, she'd smile and laugh. Sometimes, she'd choke up and cry. But she felt young again, almost normal again.

That afternoon, after talking herself out, she went back to where the garden used to be, where her dad had taught her everything she knew about planting, watering, and growing. When she reached the garden, though, she did a double-take. On the ground was a box filled with dirt. The garden was back. Lena looked around, cautiously. Her father was real?

Lena broke into a huge grin, squealed like a mouse, then covered her mouth. She worked on the tiny garden all afternoon as bystanders gawked and mocked. She didn't care. She loved her father, and this garden was now the closest thing she had to him.

"Come on, Lena," a familiar voice called. Lena turned around. It was Trix, and the expression on his face said it all. "You're not a child anymore. It's time to stop letting your imagination get the better of you. Get out of whoever's yard you're in. You don't have a dad."

Lena looked at the garden, then back at Trix. "My father put this here for me—isn't it wonderful, Mr. Trix?"

"Yeah," Trix mocked. "I'm sure you'll be thinking that when the storm comes in tonight and you catch hypothermia."

Dark clouds were already rolling in. "But it's so beautiful out here," Lena said.

"Have it your way," Trix said, waving his hand. Lena watched him walk down the driveway and disappear into his house down the street.

When she turned back to the garden, she couldn't believe her eyes. The house was back. Everything was back. But where was Father? Lena ran all over, looking frantically for him.

After exhausting every place she knew to look, she trudged to where the bench had been. And while the bench was there again, her father wasn't. All of the excitement suddenly crushed inside her. She sat on the bench and—

Wait. Her feet. They were dangling off the bench instead of touching the ground. She was small again.

"Room for two here?" her father said, approaching from behind. Lena smiled so broadly that she couldn't speak. She patted his side of the bench and her father sat down. She snuggled close to make sure he was real.

"What happened to the house and everything, Daddy?" Lena asked.

"Oh, it's all fine. You were just too big to see it for a while."

Lena squinted, thinking about what he meant.

"Is it okay if I stay this size forever?" she said.

Her father laughed. "Sounds good to me."

3 Pillars of Childlikeness

Lena talked about her dad all the time. He was real to her. That's how God wants us to be. Because when we're drawn away from our heavenly Father, as Lena was to Trix's house, we grow up in a sense. We become adultlike. And when we're adultlike, we're too big to see God.

Childlikeness—even though it looks like foolishness, such as talking to someone who isn't there, or getting excited about a garden box—has the opposite effect. It unashamedly praises God every day, in front of anyone, for whatever reason, gushing about how he is so big, so mighty, and *how could he ever love me, and why would he ever save me,* and *oh God is amazingly good.*

Now, take a look at the DNA of childlikeness—the very elements that, when pressed together and stirred in your heart, make you childlike: humility, trust, and abandonment to Jesus Christ.

Humbly Lose Yourself in the Depths of Your Father

> I will extol you, my God and King, and bless your name forever and ever. Every day I will bless you and praise your name forever and ever. Great is the Lord, and greatly to be praised, and his greatness is unsearchable (Psalm 145:1-3).

When children see a skyscraper, they show no shame in tilting their heads back and staring. The building is huge! They recognize just how abnormally big the building is compared to everything else. They smile and beg Mom and Dad to look too. But the parents, of course, don't stop to admire. They're used to the skyscraper.

So it is with God.

Whereas our inner adult mentally cuts God down to whatever size suits us, children respond to God and all of his bigness with awe and wonder. In order to be childlike, you must lose yourself in the depths of God as your Father: his mind, his hands, his feet, his heart, his clothes, his home.

His mind. Be like the child who unashamedly says, "My daddy always has the answer. He never has to look up anything. He knows what I mean even when I don't know what I mean." Lose yourself in the fact that his thoughts are above your thoughts, and his ways above your ways.

His hands. Be like the child who says, "My daddy makes everything all by himself. Look over here—he made that! And look over here—he made this too!" Lose yourself in the fact that all of creation is declaring the glory of God and pouring out the richness of his character. And that no matter where you are, or who you're with, or what your circumstance—you can see, hear, and know God through what he's made.

His feet. Be like the child who says, "My daddy has the best job in the world. He heals people who are sick and dying." Lose yourself in the fact that God is busy in our world, working all things together for the good of his children and drawing lost souls to himself.

His heart. Be like the child who says, "My daddy loves me so much! I can get in the worst trouble and even throw rocks at my neighbor's house, but he still loves me." Lose yourself in the fact that God's love knows no bounds, that he loves you so much that he sent his only Son to die for you, and that he loves you no matter what you've done.

His clothes. Be like the child who says, "My daddy never gets dirt on his clothes. I get crayons and spaghetti on mine all the time, but dad's clothes are always so white." Lose yourself in the fact that God is perfect and holy, and that everything he does is wonderful.

His home. Be like the child who says, "My daddy is so generous with his house. He made a room just for me and he invites others to be his sons and daughters and promises to make rooms for them too!" Lose yourself in the fact that God's blessings are eternally incredible and that he's made homes for each of us.

The magnificence and bigness of God has never once shrunk in the history of the universe. The only thing that has ever shrunk is our accurate perception of him. So tilt your head back and stare. Invite the world passing by to behold the wonder with you. Be a child among adults as you infiltrate.

Trust Your Father No Matter How Great or Grim Your Circumstances Are

> Therefore I tell you, do not be anxious about your life, what you will eat or what you will drink, nor about your body, what you will put on. Is not life more than food, and the body more than clothing? Look at the birds of the air: they neither sow nor reap nor gather into barns, and yet your heavenly Father feeds them. Are you not of more value than they? And which of you by being anxious can add a single hour to his span of life? (Matthew 6:25-27).

If a father picks up his child and starts flinging him into the air, the child laughs. If the father is in the pool, the child will jump in too. Children know they're protected when they're with their daddy.

Imagine doing the kinds of things that would normally freak you out, *knowing* that you're safe.

In Daniel 3, Shadrach, Meshach, and Abednego are standing in front of a king who's ready to burn off their faces, shouting, "And who is the god who will deliver you from my hands?" But the three of them calmly and confidently refused to worship King Nebuchadnezzar's image of gold. One of them even said:

"O Nebuchadnezzar, we have no need to answer you in this matter. If this be so, our God whom we serve is able to deliver us from the burning fiery furnace, and he will deliver us out of your hand, O king. But if not, let it be known to you, O king, that we will not serve your gods or worship the golden image that you have set up" (Daniel 3:16-18).

> We may see a risk as unsettling, perhaps frightening, but when we are deep in the center of God's will, even a risk is safe.[5]
>
> Wayne Cordeiro

The three of them trusted that they were safe because they knew—regardless of whether or not the king burned them alive—that God was with them.

When we're childlike enough to trust that we're safe with God, no matter what, we can do anything. It doesn't matter how difficult the task. It doesn't matter if you don't think you have what it takes. It doesn't matter if people don't think anything of you. It doesn't matter if your life is crumbling. It doesn't matter if you're weak.

It also doesn't matter how uncommitted to Christ you've been in your past. One friend puts it like this:

"Noah was a drunk, Abraham was too old, Isaac was a daydreamer, Jacob was a liar, Leah was ugly, Joseph was abused, Moses had a stuttering problem, Gideon was afraid, Samson was a womanizer, Rahab was a prostitute, Jeremiah and Timothy were too young, David had an affair and was a murderer, Elijah was suicidal, Isaiah preached naked, Jonah ran from God, Naomi was a widow, Job went bankrupt, the disciples fell asleep while praying, the Samaritan woman was divorced, Zacchaeus was too small, Paul was too religious, Timothy had an ulcer, and Lazarus was dead. Do you seriously think God can't use you?"

If God calls you to something that seems impossible, he'll strengthen you to accomplish it. Infiltrate knowing that you are always safe with God.

Live Abandoned to Your Father

> Are your most passionate expressions in a given week directed toward the Lover of your soul?[6]
>
> James MacDonald

Children trust their father. They want to be with him. They wonder at his bigness. They brag on him. They say ridiculously real things to him. They cling to his leg. They cry over wrong things they've done against him. They hang on his every word. They believe they can do anything with him.

They're abandoned to him.

Does that describe your relationship to God? Or does the inner adult in you question his authority, think about its own bigness, hold its tongue from praising him, listen sparingly, avoid awkward closeness, and get defensive when it's done wrong against him? These are signs of our inner adults invading us.

Living abandoned to Jesus sets us free to be who we're meant to be: untied from conformity, freed from pride, and empowered to liberate others. But abandonment doesn't come naturally. It comes gradually. It's a process of shrinking from adults into children. And it's an active step. A choice. A lifestyle Infiltrators must intentionally pursue.

> The Holy Spirit loves to work in an environment of genuine affection, where people know that the larger goal is not about them; it's about the Messiah being born, it's about Christ coming into the world, it's about eternity invading our lives. That's where the excitement is.[7]
>
> Wayne Cordeiro

An abandoned person prays without stopping, because who doesn't want to talk with their father?

An abandoned person flows with love for God no matter who's around, because who isn't enthralled with his daddy?

An abandoned person can't wait to hear his daddy speak, because who refuses a great redemption story?

An abandoned person gazes at him and is overcome by who his daddy is, because who doesn't admire perfection?

An abandoned person lets go of everything he once held on to, because what's worth holding on to but his daddy?

An abandoned person thinks about God and everything he's done for us, because who isn't astonished by love and kindness?

An abandoned person believes he can do anything with daddy by his side—*anything*—because who isn't full of hope when in the presence of their king?

> You have a destiny, but your destiny is fulfilled by investing in the destinies of others.[8]
>
> Stephen Mansfield

Do you feel the child inside you right now, maybe caged up, teary-eyed, beaten and bony? It's time to set this captive free. It's time to become childlike and infiltrate in a way that will liberate your brothers and sisters to live with humility, trust, and abandonment to Jesus.

Turn and Become Like Children

> Well done, good and faithful servant. You have been faithful over a little; I will set you over much. Enter into the joy of your master (Matthew 25:21).

It might be hard to imagine now, but one day our time on earth will end and we will actually meet Jesus. What we first believed without seeing, we'll see with our own eyes. All of the doubts and insecurities that tortured us will seem strangely insignificant. Our entire sense of what's important will vanish. We'll realize that life after death is real. And that God's promises were true all along. And that every morsel of ourselves we gave up for Christ…we didn't give in vain.

Then the ultimate realization will shake us to the core: We're about to meet the king of the universe, Jesus Christ.

In that moment, I can only visualize one of two emotions: that of utter anticipation and hope, or that of anxiety and loss. We will have either served and known Christ so intimately on earth that seeing him will be like a grandiose reunion, or we will have ignored him and presumed upon his friendship so much that seeing him will be like meeting a person who took a bullet for us only to see us not care.

> Would you consider yourself ready to meet God this afternoon or before bed tonight? What kind of impact would the gravity of that revelation make on your plans for the day?[9]
>
> Ed Stetzer

God tells us that the gate is narrow that leads to life, and that those who find it are few. We know that our inner adult, who's caught up in pride and conformity, is not fit for the kingdom of heaven. So where does that leave us?

"Turn," Jesus says, "and become like children."

What Now?

Watch this chapter's video at www.calledtostay.com.

Get the download of "3 Pillars of Childlikeness" here: www.called tostay.com.

"I was childlike today when I…" — Post this as your Facebook status and I'll join the conversation (just remember to tag me).

What's Next

We've discovered why we must stay in the church. We've looked at how to equip ourselves. Now it's time to discover what we must do in the church.

The body of Christ is filled with people wandering away from the truth of Scripture and the true call of Jesus. Infiltration is about bringing people back to truth. Back to commitment. Back to conviction.

Discovering how to do that is next.

CHAPTER 7

How to Infiltrate —One

Be Intentional and Intuitive

> My brothers, if anyone among you wanders from the truth and someone brings him back, let him know that whoever brings back a sinner from his wandering will save his soul from death and will cover a multitude of sins (James 5:19-20).

I knew it was working when my friend started taking notes on a napkin as we talked about devotion to Jesus.

I knew it was working when a fellow believer lit up as God nudged my wife and me to speak openly about what true faithfulness to Jesus looks like.

I knew it was working when, after a book study with dozens of mature Christians, a young man went out of his way to say, "Your words tonight carried more weight than everything else combined. My heart cries with yours."

The enemy would like us to use experiences like these to puff up our pride, as if we are the reason things are stirring. But this is infiltration. This is the power of Jesus working in his church through those who answer his call.

In order to help believers move toward total commitment to Jesus, we must be intentional and intuitive. That's what this chapter is about.

We're going to explore how to "proclaim liberty to the captives and recovering of sight to the blind" (Luke 4:18).

This means making yourself a slave to helping others progress in their walk with Jesus. It means becoming electric to the stagnant, committed to the withdrawn, fearless to the fearful, loving to the judgmental, giving to the consumer, and accepting to the rejecting (1 Corinthians 9:19-23).

It means clothing yourself with compassion, kindness, humility, gentleness, and patience, not only putting up with each other's quirks, but accepting them as well.

> The mark of Jesus is love, costly love, and it does not come naturally or easily.[1]
>
> Timothy George and John Woodbridge

And forgiving freely. And most of all, doing all things in love, which binds us in unity (Colossians 3:12-14).

It means letting the peace of Jesus rule in your heart. And being thankful. And letting the message of Christ dwell in you richly as you teach and admonish others (Colossians 3:15-16).

It means gently restoring people who are caught in the various sins of the church and carrying each other's burdens, being careful that you yourself aren't led astray (Galatians 6:1-2).

It means doing everything the best you can in order to help the weak, remembering the words Jesus himself said: "It is more blessed to give than to receive" (Acts 20:35).

It means warning those who are idle and disruptive in the church, encouraging those who are disheartened, helping the weak, and being patient with everyone (1 Thessalonians 5:14).

It means thinking modestly of yourself and with sober judgment so you'll never become conceited as though you were God's gift to ugly church people (Romans 12:3).

And it means accepting the one whose faith is weak without quarreling over disputable matters (Romans 14:1). It means seeking good for others, not yourself (1 Corinthians 10:24). And it means bearing with the failings of the weak in a way that's not just pleasing to yourself (Romans 15:1). Because "whoever thus serves Christ is acceptable to God and approved by men" (Romans 14:18).

The Story of Justin, Christi, and Haley

In an instant, Justin realized that his suspicions were true: His wife, Christi, was cheating on him. Whether emotionally or physically, he didn't know. But what did it matter? His heart was broken.

When Justin approached Christi about it, she cussed him out for his snoopiness and even spit on his face. She accused him of having an affair first, which couldn't have been further from the truth. Her words cut Justin so badly that he couldn't even speak. He simply left the room.

Christi quit trying to hide her feelings for her secret lovers. She lived her life in the open and asked Justin every day when he'd file for divorce. He never answered.

> Great men and women of God are not exempt from hurt and offense...Indeed, it seems that the greater a man is in God, the more opposition from fellow believers he is forced to endure.[2]
>
> Stephen Mansfield

For weeks, Justin poured himself into loving Christi, writing her love letters, texting her how much he loved her, cooking dinner, cleaning the house, leaving her gifts, and doing his best to show her affection. But nothing changed. The only time she even spoke to him was when she wanted to vent about Haley, one of her friends who apparently had "gone nuts" on her—whatever that meant.

One day, while Christi was on a jog, Justin paced around the house in panic. He didn't know what else to do. He grabbed Christi's cell, not really knowing what he was looking for. He opened her address book.

Name after name made him groan. He'd met nearly all of these people and knew they'd be no help in winning Christi back. But then he came across the name Haley. He decided she might be his only chance to get through to Christi. So he dialed the number.

"Hello?" Haley answered.

"Hi. This is Justin—Christi's husband."

Silence.

"This is strange, but I was hoping you could help me. It's about Christi."

Justin spent the next five minutes expressing his love for his wife, even breaking into tears. He'd forgotten how amazing it felt to express his love for her to someone. He almost forgot that Haley was on the other line. Nothing in the world seemed to matter.

When he finished, silence again filled the line. "Please," Justin said. "Would you just…tell her that for me?" He broke down, sobbing, and hung up, feeling both exposed and childish.

A few weeks later, while making coffee, Christi came up behind Justin and reached for her mug. As she did, though, she brushed her cheek to his and said, "Thank you."

Justin turned, stunned. But Christi was already heading out the door with her coffee. He couldn't believe what had just happened. As he paced about in the kitchen, ecstatic, his gaze landed on the fridge calendar. Circled on that day's date were the same words that marked every second Friday of the month: *Girls' Night Out.*

Horror immediately filled his chest. Every time Christi went out with friends, she'd come back home doubly angry with him.

He sat on the living room couch in near darkness from the moment Christi left. He didn't eat anything or drink anything. He simply sat and stared into blackness.

Justin woke up at midnight, but wasn't sure why. He was still on the couch. Must have fallen asleep. He heard shoes slip off in the entryway and steps coming his way. It was odd that Christi was home before 4 a.m. She sat down, leaned over, and kissed him on the cheek.

"Can we talk?" she said.

Justin sat up and the two of them talked into the night about their marriage. Christi teared up about her affair and asked if Justin would give her a chance to fulfill her vows. Justin could hardly speak. He wrapped Christi into his arms and held her. Both of them cried for what seemed like an hour.

When they finally pulled away from each other, Justin asked, "What's changed?"

"I had a fight with Haley," she said. "She'd read some of your text messages and confronted me about them because I'd been telling everyone that you were verbally abusive to me. After that we started talking about our marriage more often—especially about how I was making you look awful."

Christi continued: "My other friends found out what was going on. They all got mad at Haley at first, but then they saw what was really happening and sided with her. Then tonight, we all talked. I broke down. And now I'm here."

Their marriage began to heal. They spent more time with each other, and less with everyone else.

One day, while Haley was over for dinner, Christi asked her, "Why did you do what you did for us?"

"Because I could see what you were missing out on," Haley responded. "And I wanted you to have it."

If Justin represents Jesus and Christi represents the church, then we are Haley and Christi's friends. We have a great, constant influence on the church. We either misguidedly encourage her to go against her loving husband or, like Haley, we see things for how they truly are and show the church that she's slandering her husband.

It's not popular, and others in the church might not like us for a time—or ever—but it eventually leads to making the bride beautiful for Christ.

Haley exemplifies the three inner resolutions every Infiltrator must rise to:

- Respond to the call
- Endure the heartache
- Share the good life

Respond to the Call

> And I heard the voice of the Lord saying, "Whom shall I send, and who will go for us?" Then I said, "Here I am! Send me" (Isaiah 6:8).

Haley didn't know of Christi's horrible wrongs against her husband until she received Justin's call and heard him out.

Today, there are so many believers blindly encouraging the church's divorce of Jesus.

We hang out at church. We do church talk. But every time we get that call, that feeling from the Holy Spirit telling us that there's more to church than this, we dismiss it. We think it's unrealistic or flat-out utopian.

We need to be like Haley and respond to the call. This is the first resolution of an Infiltrator.

Endure the Heartache

> We who are strong have an obligation to bear with the failings of the weak, and not to please ourselves. Let each of us please his neighbor for his good, to build him up. For Christ did not please himself, but as it is written, "The reproaches of those who reproached you fell on me" (Romans 15:1-3).

The second resolution of an Infiltrator is to endure the heartache.

Christi and her friends berated Haley—even though Haley was *right*. In our day and age of victimhood, it would be easy for Haley to just dump Christi and the rest of the friends. Why not? They treated her like dirt. She should go find friends who respect her more. That's how we're trained to think.

But the Bible teaches us different. It says we should bear with sinners. Forgive them. And love them. That's what Haley did. She stayed true and, eventually, the other friends and Christi saw she was right.

This second resolution is the hardest part of infiltration. But those who endure it play a vital, influential role in the lives of their brothers and sisters.

Share the Good Life

> I do it all for the sake of the gospel, that I may share with them in its blessings (1 Corinthians 9:23).

Christ-inspired goodness and sacrifice, when done with a smile and a genuine desire to bless and spread blessing, almost always send a message that can't be preached in a Sunday sermon.[3]

Ed Stetzer

Despite responding to the call of passionate commitment and enduring the heartache, the most important thing we learn from Haley is her motive, which is the third resolution of an infiltrator: to share the good life.

Haley didn't do what she did for personal gain. She didn't do it because she liked sticking her nose into other people's business. She didn't endure the pain just for the sake of suffering for what's right. She didn't do it so she could hold it over her friends' heads when the truth was revealed.

She did it for no other reason than wanting the very best for her friend. This is the third and final resolution of an Infiltrator.

Your deep desire to respond to the call, endure the heartache, and share the good life equips you for the infiltration to come.

Evaluate Your Church

We will not answer to God as a collective whole, but as individuals. This means that it doesn't matter how healthy or sick the body of Christ is at the end of our days. It matters what each of us has done to make her healthier or sicker.

> Human love is directed to the other person for his own sake, spiritual love loves him for Christ's sake.[4]
>
> Dietrich Bonhoeffer

The rest of this chapter is dedicated to the steps you can start taking toward making her healthier.

The first step to moving your church toward a greater commitment to Jesus is to discover what's holding it back. To do this, you need to look at your church through four different lenses: its love for Jesus, its obedience to Jesus, its trust in Jesus, and its knowledge of Jesus.

> If you are passionate about the people and community where God has sent you, and if you love them as He does, you will be motivated to know and understand their story.[5]
>
> Ed Stetzer

In the space provided, write in a number that describes your church. Use 0 for "not at all," 1 for "somewhat," 2 for "mostly," and 3 for "very much."

Your Church's Love for Jesus

> And he said to him, "You shall love the Lord your God with
> all your heart and with all your soul and with all your mind"
> (Matthew 22:37).

People at my church are verbally affectionate for Jesus. They adore
Jesus. You can see it in their eyes. You can hear it in their voices. There
is no one on earth they speak of so highly. No one on earth they'd
rather talk about. No one on earth who holds their hearts like King
Jesus. When they pray, they do not pray for the benefit of those around
them. They talk directly with God the Father—like a child talking to a
famous role model. They never have to say that Jesus is the main thing
to them. He's obviously the main thing to them.

_____

People at my church show adoration for Jesus in worship. They
gather for worship with a great sense of anticipation. You can tell they're
coming together into the very presence of the God who knit their souls
and spun their beautiful world into existence. You can tell they're coming together into the presence of the only person on earth worthy of
unreserved worship. One who is worthy of their closed eyes, lifted
hands, bowed heads, or bent knees. You can tell they come together
desiring a taste of the heavenly country that God has prepared.

_____

People at my church desire for others to know Jesus. They long for
unbelievers to know him. The thought of someone separated from
Christ stabs their hearts because they cannot imagine life apart from
the abundant hope and joy and love they share in him. They pour
themselves out to God in prayer, pleading that the hearts of people
would melt before him, and that those who do not know him would
find him.

_____

Total: _____

Your Church's Obedience to Jesus

If you love me, you will keep my commandments (John 14:15).

People at my church love and serve others. They not only look to meet others' needs emotionally and physically as they arise, but they plan on it as well. Their calendars reflect a lifestyle of putting others before themselves. There is so much that goes on that only God sees: serving the homeless, cooking meals and bringing food to those who are lacking, visiting with the lonely and outcast, singing for the joyless, weeping with the broken, rejoicing with the happy, lending a hand to those who are overworked, and hugging those in pain.

_____

People at my church practice forgiveness and make peace. They don't put a limit on their grace and forgiveness toward others, just as Jesus didn't put a limit on his grace and forgiveness of them. They forgive their brothers' and sisters' sins seven times seventy times and deal straightforwardly with those who wrong them, unwilling to have relationships that are little more than coexistence and bitterness. When people attack their personal dignity or deal unfairly with them, they give up their personal rights for the sake of Jesus.

_____

People at my church tell others about Jesus. They eagerly look to make disciples of everyone around them. Their church is mission control, and going into the world every day is their mission. They give up their comfort, their desires, and their image for the sake of loving others to Jesus, who gave up his comfort and desires and image for us. They're so caught up in what Christ has given them that they want to give their all to Christ's mission of bringing people to himself. They talk about Jesus to anyone and everyone, even those who intimidate them. They know that those who acknowledge Jesus before all the people of the earth will one day be acknowledged by Jesus before God in heaven.

_____

Total: _____

Your Church's Trust in Jesus

> Trust in the Lord with all your heart, and do not lean on
> your own understanding (Proverbs 3:5).

People at my church get out of their comfort zones. They do daring things for Jesus, even if it means putting themselves into situations where they're bound to get backlash. They are not afraid of those who can kill the body but cannot kill the soul. They cling to the great peace of knowing that Jesus is with them to the end of time. Too much comfort is almost uncomfortable to them. They enjoy the comfort God gives, of course, but they grow uneasy if they start getting the feeling that they don't need God to show up for them to be okay. They know their life here isn't about sitting in comfort, but following Jesus regardless of discomfort.

_____

People at my church rely on the power of the Holy Spirit and prayer. They don't worry about what to say about Jesus or how to say it when they're in a bind. They know it won't be them speaking, but the Spirit of God speaking through them. They are in constant prayer, asking God for things that will help them carry out his will. They know there are no limits on their prayers, and that is how they pray. They believe God will answer according to his good purposes, and that being in prayer keeps them away from the temptations of the world.

_____

People at my church are uplifted by God's promises. They are always lifted up by God's promise to them of a future and a hope, rest for their souls, power and strength, and the unbreakable love of God. They are amazing when it comes to being glad—no matter what. When people insult them for loving Jesus, they keep their heads up knowing that he's promised to reward their suffering. When they face trouble and hardships of all kinds, they consider it a joy because they know that the stretching of their faith makes them stronger, and that God ultimately will make them mature and complete through it.

_____

Total: _____

Your Church's Knowledge of Jesus

> All Scripture is breathed out by God and profitable for teaching, for reproof, for correction, and for training in righteousness (2 Timothy 3:16).

People at my church study the whole truth of the Bible. They are careful to study not just some truths about God, but all of them. They don't dismiss the wrath of God while studying the love of God. They don't neglect the sovereignty of God while studying their personal responsibility in life. They don't neglect God's call to be holy while studying his abundant mercy and grace. They just do their best to understand God and his plan for them so they can live with greater conviction and obedience.

_____

People at my church don't ignore the life of Jesus in the context of Scripture. They don't get so caught up in theology that they lose sight of the example of Jesus, who said, "Anyone who has seen me has seen the Father" (John 14:9). They talk just as often of his parables, actions, and ministry as they do of doctrine, and aim to live as reflections of both. It's not uncommon for conversations to go back and forth between the life of Jesus, the writings of Paul and the apostles, and the Old Testament. It isn't that some words in the Bible are less inspired than others to them. It's that they never want to forget that Jesus is the rock of their salvation, not a stagnant centerpiece of their religion.

> Have you ever deliberately looked at every function of your church through the grid of its mission?[6]
>
> Wayne Cordeiro

_____

People at my church focus on the ultimate purpose of Scripture. They don't get bogged down by endless bouts of too much work (legalism) versus too much grace (licentiousness). They don't get caught up in denominational squabbles. They instead look to their ultimate purpose of loving God and others, glorifying God and enjoying him forever, doing justice, loving mercy, and walking humbly.

_____

Total: _____

Now, add up your four totals from above into one grand total:

_____

Here's a general idea of what your grand total means:

31–36

You are a part of a church where God is doing an incredible work. Your work as an Infiltrator will be full-on enjoyable and life-giving. Keep shining for Christ and never tire of showering this world with love. We need more churches like yours.

23–30

You are a part of a blessed church that's making strides toward Christlikeness that many churches don't. Your work as an Infiltrator will most likely focus on one specific area that's holding your church back. Make it your mission to step out and stretch yourself for Jesus in this area—even if you get some cockeyed looks. Don't focus on results. Just focus on being consistent, which subtly breaks down any walls that exist. A church-wide deeper commitment to Jesus is a real possibility for your church.

15–22

You are a part of a church that's operating in a mix of faith and fear. There's a chance that the followers in your church have settled into consumerism, eating up spirituality while hiding their lights from our dark world. But there's an equally good chance that they do not know what they are doing and just need someone to help show them the full way of Jesus. Humbly and fearlessly be that person. Make it your goal to stir up conviction and point others to Christ. You'll experience a good amount of frustration—and church-wide change will seem like a long, difficult road—but you'll be encouraged by the deeper relationships and personal commitments to Jesus that form out of your infiltration.

7–14

You are a part of a church that breaks your heart. It's stuck in mediocrity and no one seems to notice. You wonder if there's any hope for it. The answer is *yes*...But that hope is intimately connected to you and people like you—those who love Jesus and are fully devoted to him, but feel suffocated in church. Your work as Infiltrators, if you stay, will be painful. You will be misunderstood and most likely looked at as a threat. But if God gives you the will to help other individuals overcome their lukewarmness, you will be greatly blessed. You can offer yourself to God in his work of making your brothers and sisters more like Jesus—and dramatically alter the course of their lives.

0–6

You are a part of a dead church. The pastor is not a true shepherd, and most likely every effort of infiltration will be akin to throwing pearls before swine. With no intention of glorifying God, this church may be one you should leave unless you feel sure you're supposed to stay. If God moves you to stay, keep on the lookout for seekers: those who do not know much about Jesus but are looking. God may be keeping you there to meet one of these and help move them toward Christ.

> God calls us to repent of our critical spirit and pick up one of concern instead. Genuine concern is what happens when we see a problem and we care. That kind of concern leads to positive changes for us and our church.[7]
>
> Joshua Harris

3 Ways to Mentally Prepare for Infiltration

Everything to this point hasn't actually touched on that moment you walk into your church for the first time having decided to infiltrate.

We haven't discussed what to do when you're standing in the middle of the greeting area at your church, and everything you remember about the atmosphere is the same, and an overwhelming sense of hopelessness smashes into whatever inspiration you had before you darkened the doorway of your church. That moment is monumental.

If you cannot get through it, you'll never experience the awesomeness of infiltration.

How do you get through? There is one thing that helps tremendously: mentally minimizing your church.

If your church seems like an impenetrable fortress, filled with people who are set in their spiritual ways, the first thing you need to do is make it small in your mind. Not small as in insignificant. But small in that God's plans for his bride are so far beyond your one church, in your one town, in your one corner of the world.

Making your church small in your mind is like revisiting your old high school: You can't believe how big it used to be to you before you grew up and discovered life existed after senior year.

To minimize your church, it's vital that you get well acquainted with the global church. The absolute best ways I know to do this are attending Christian conferences, reading good books, and actively looking to experience your faith.

Conferences

Conferences break down the walls we mentally construct in our own minds about our home churches. They help us do this through connecting us to a diverse group of believers.

Conference mealtimes are underrated. Sometimes, they can be more valuable than the main sessions—because they're a microcosm of the global church. My wife and I have shared lunches and dinners with people from all over the country and from all different kinds of Christian backgrounds. It's amazing what you and your fellow believers can talk about when the walls of each person's background crumble away. This is one of the best parts of conferences.

Such conversations show you the different ways God is at work in his church. It reveals just how broad his canvas and how large his paintbrushes really are. Best of all, it makes your home church's impenetrable walls seem smaller and smaller, and stirs up more and more boldness inside you to jump them.

Bringing together Christians from all different walks of life makes for a beautiful worship experience. Because there are no unspoken rules directing the flow of praise to God.

To the right, there are people lifting their hands and straining their voices for their king. To the left, there are those kneeling and shedding tears. A few rows up are couples simply closing their eyes and holding hands as they lift their voices to Jesus. And toward the front and back, some are dancing as an expression of worship.

Diversity of worship breaks the uniformity many of us grow used to in our home churches. It stirs your heart to see the beauty of God's reach into his individual children's souls. It builds in you a clearer vision of the tremendously huge redemption story he's orchestrating throughout the earth.

This kind of grand beauty is a taste of heaven and leaves us wanting more. And by getting us caught up in our heavenly country, we minimize the fear in our earthly one.

Including the fear we feel at our home church.

If you've grown up in one or two churches, you can get desensitized to whoever's in the pulpit. From the books your pastor spends the most time preaching from to the way he uses voice inflection, it becomes old hat. This can be a bad thing if you let it. It can subtly lead you into thinking that your pastor is *the* pastor, kind of like the people in the Corinthian church thought their pastor was *the* pastor (1 Corinthians 1:12).

There's nothing wrong with loving your pastor and speaking highly of him. I speak very highly of my pastors. But if your pastor or pastors become a sort of standard of excellence in your mind, the idea of infiltrating their church seems almost offensive. A little voice in your head protests: "Who are you to think you can help stir people toward Christ when we have the best pastor in the pulpit?" It makes your church seem big and impenetrable.

When you go to a conference, you hear from all sorts of different pastors and teachers, all of whom bring a different flavor to the proclamation of God's Word. And by hearing from all sorts of godly men and women, your pastor back home shrinks from *the* pastor to just your pastor. This, too, helps minimize a wall in your church.

When we connect with fellow brothers and sisters at conferences and take in the amazing diversity of God's family, we're left with several impressions on our souls that never go away. These impressions are our allies for life as Infiltrators.

I cannot count the times I've walked into my church, felt the weight of its bigness, and then subconsciously recalled one of the conference's impressions inside me. Sometimes it's of a conversation I had with someone who astounded me with his or her faith, or love, or intimacy with Jesus. Sometimes it's of an experience I had when someone offered to pray over me on the spot. Or a mental picture of the unity shared among believers who might not agree on every theological issue, but who love each other like true brothers and sisters nonetheless.

Impressions are like memories made of gunpowder. When you're overcome by the bigness of your church, they come to your aide, ready to blast a hole so you can infiltrate.

Instead of finding yourself paralyzed, you're amped up by impressions of what the bride of Christ can be. Instead of feeling lost and overwhelmed by all of your fellow believers around you, you're moved to bring them the good life in Jesus.

Yes, conferences can be expensive, but the time spent mingling with other Christians from around the globe and experiencing things that help you mentally minimize your church are worth it. Make a point of making it to at least one conference a year. Raise the money if you have to. As an Infiltrator, you won't regret it.

> For in one Spirit we were all baptized into one body—Jews or Greeks, slaves or free—and all were made to drink of one Spirit. For the body does not consist of one member but of many...If all were a single member, where would the body be? (1 Corinthians 12:13-14,19).

Literature

Reading the literature of believers (within the realm of what's scriptural) is another great way to minimize your church. Reading books and blogs from numerous people with numerous missions and visions is like going away to college: It refines your faith and has the potential of growing you more than in any other time in your life.

The key word there is *potential*.

Going away to college can also destroy someone's faith, as silver-tongued professors wax eloquent about Christianity's triteness. So while owning your faith amid the fire of different worldviews (or biblical views) skyrockets your confidence in Christ, it doesn't come without risks. Consider this the caveat of minimizing your church in this way.

Reading Christian literature—again, within the realms of what glorifies God—minimizes your church in that you see how much bigger Christianity is outside of your church's pulpit. You become free to think and come to conclusions about your beliefs while warding off the danger of blindly adhering to every word that comes out of your pastor's mouth (without giving it thought and evaluation yourself).

You will no doubt come across some writers and thinkers you don't agree with. But in that non-agreement you cement your own faith in Jesus. You no longer shy away from infiltrating with authority. Because there no longer remain those questions that stilt your confidence. There no longer remain those moments when you wonder, *Maybe I really don't know what I'm talking about. Maybe there's something I just don't get.* You've immersed yourself in all of the conversations happening regarding Christianity. You've been forced to think through biblical things that, most likely, others in your church have not.

You're going to come across error and ill advice, and you're going to come across gold that encourages your walk with Jesus. Discernment is a gift from God we all must employ to the fullest when mentally minimizing our churches.

That said, keep these three things in mind:

- Read writers and thinkers who challenge your natural conservative or liberal bent. This makes for excellent iron sharpening iron (Proverbs 27:17).

- Read writers and thinkers who mirror Jesus. Those who exude humility, love believers and nonbelievers alike, and strive to learn more about God—not just be right. Avoid those who come across as hostile or arrogant. Their ideas are not worth their poisonous attitudes.

• Engage in the discussions on social media every once in a while. When you have questions, comment. When something doesn't seem right to you but no one has said anything, write what you're feeling. See who says what, then test what's said.

Oh how I love your law! It is my meditation all the day…I have more understanding than all my teachers, for your testimonies are my meditation. I understand more than the aged, for I keep your precepts. I hold back my feet from every evil way, in order to keep your word. I do not turn aside from your rules, for you have taught me. How sweet are your words to my taste, sweeter than honey to my mouth! (Psalm 119:97,99-103).

Experience

To infiltrate powerfully, you need street cred, if you will. It's hard to point others toward commitment to Jesus if it's all just in your head.

We cannot stir up love for Jesus in others if we do not overflow with love for him ourselves. We cannot encourage the importance of obedience to Jesus if we ourselves do not take his commands seriously. We cannot set a tone of trust in Jesus if we ourselves never go out on a limb as his disciples did. And we cannot push an agenda of knowing more about Jesus and the ways of God if we haven't immersed ourselves in studies ourselves.

Lack of experience limits your ability to infiltrate. You have to choose what you're best suited for.

I come from a knowledge background. I lacked love and trust. These are the kinds of believers I'm most capable of infiltrating. I know how they think because I know how I thought. I know what they're blind to because I know what I was blind to. I know what will help them move toward Jesus because I know what helped me move toward Jesus.

This doesn't mean you have to have loads of experience. It just means that you must genuinely be walking the walk, not just talking the talk. It's another way of taking the plank out of your own eye before trying to remove the speck in your brother's.

Are you living the life you're trying to inject into others? If you cannot say with conviction that you are, then meet with Jesus. Consider diving back into the chapter "Where to Start," opening your heart and soul to God, and seeing how he moves in you.

> What good is it, my brothers, if someone says he has faith but does not have works?...For as the body apart from the spirit is dead, so also faith apart from works is dead (James 2:14,26).

Find the Red Apples

A year or two into our marriage, my wife and I were invited to watch a presentation at someone's home. A moneymaking opportunity, we were told. Before long, we discovered that it wasn't so much about a way to make money as it was a way for others to make money off us. But we learned something of value that day.

> If life transformation is the goal, recruit those who show a clear and current pattern of transformation in their lives and who love to know and apply theological truths.[8]
>
> Ed Stetzer

The difference between green apples and red apples.

Green apples, the presenter said, were people we wanted to avoid. Green apple people ask too many questions and make decisions at a snail's pace. Their first reaction to opportunity is skepticism rather than excitement.

Red apples, on the other hand, catch the vision of what the presenter is selling right away. They jump aboard the thrill train from the get-go and rush forward with all the thrill of a lottery winner.

While I'll never be a big fan of selling or the psychology behind it, the apple concept is something that's proven itself as a foundational part of infiltrating. When you walk into a church for the first time after having decided to infiltrate, it can feel like you're all alone. An outcast. The person who refuses to fit in like everyone else. It can be a real psychological challenge, as we just explored.

Red apples give the Infiltrator hope.

Red apples are those in your church who've struck you as someone ripe for deeper commitment to Jesus. Maybe it was something they said in a conversation, or at a book study, or perhaps something they posted on social media.

However it may have come, it triggered you to think that the person has a longing in their soul. You got the sense that something was nagging at their heart. That they knew there was more to following Jesus and experiencing God than this.

Pinpoint these people in your church. They are your starting point. Not only are they potentially on the verge of stepping into a deeper relationship with Christ, they are also potentially life-giving and lifelong friends. They help you see that there really are people in churches today who long for more. They help you see that God uses infiltration to help individuals and, in some cases, entire churches overcome whatever it is that's standing between them and passionate commitment.

Bonding with Red Apples

Stephen W. Smith says, "Rituals give meaning to moments. They remind us that what is happening is not ordinary but significant and that we need to wake up and pay attention to what is happening around us." [9]

Communion is sacred. Communion is meant for the true believer who's given his life to Christ. Communion is for reflection on what Jesus Christ has done for us. Communion is special.

A lot of people don't like communion because of its "religious" feel. But communion isn't done in vain or without purpose. It isn't just something we do because we're Christians. God isn't counting how many times we do it. He's looking at our hearts when we're remembering him.

Try hosting a night of communion. Get out of the ordinary. Sit around a table. Pour glasses of something fancy. Light candles. Make it special.

Look each other in the eyes. Talk about Jesus the Savior and truly savor the discussion. Talk about his power. Talk about who you are in him. Proclaim his love. Sing together. Pray together. Ask for supernatural help to overcome apathy, lukewarmness, and any part of life where we tend to show lack of commitment. Weep with your brothers and sisters if you must. Know why you're on earth. Know why you believe what you believe. And pray for power on earth because it's hard. It's always hard. And it will only get harder.

Share around the table. Ask how Jesus has changed everyone in the last year. Ask what they believe about him. Ask how they've grown in him. Ask how the Spirit has spoken to them. Ask how God is using them in light of the great commandments and great commission. Ask how they're learning to love others. Ask what God's teaching them. Ask, "How's your heart?"

Slowing down together, remembering together, and reflecting together infuses tradition with conviction. Consider hosting a night of communion and reliving the beauty of salvation together.

One more thought from Stephen W. Smith: "The table creates the space for the ever-hovering Spirit to brood and foster life in our midst; life, not just full stomachs. At the table, the food becomes the medium for the message of love, acceptance, and belonging." [10]

Overcome Sin and Weakness by Laying on Hands

We live in a society that's become more and more "bubbleish." We like to remain in our bubbles, our comfort zones, our control zones. Because of this, many Christians are not fond of someone putting their hands on them.

When it comes to praying for someone, I believe in the power of hands. Not that laying your hands on someone does anything, but that the faith of putting your hands on someone does something. It grabs God's attention. It says, *This child believes in the power of prayer to you, Lord.*

And God responds, "It's about time."

Try hosting a night of prayer for each other, and humble yourselves by laying hands on others and praying over them. It doesn't have to be super formal. The only thing that matters is the hearts of those who attend.

When inviting people, emphasize the fact that it's a night for those

who are struggling with sin, and for those who are yearning for more
Jesus in their lives, and for those who want to grow in their faith.

Emphasize that everyone should come just
as they are, with a heart to go before God
with their fellow believers in Christ. And
to only pray when they feel led by the
Spirit of God.

> People need to move from
> sitting in rows to sitting in
> circles.[11]
> Ed Stetzer

Talk about who everyone is in Christ,
and then pray against those things that hinder your identity in Jesus.
Things like judgment, greed, jealousy, envy, pride, and every conceivable sin.

Getting real with your brothers and sisters, praying over them, and
vice-versa helps you dive deeper into your church body and opens the
door to infiltrate.

Trust in Yourself (Because God Is There)

> Let no one despise you for your youth, but set the believ-
> ers an example in speech, in conduct, in love, in faith, in
> purity…Keep a close watch on yourself and on the teach-
> ing. Persist in this, for by so doing you will save both your-
> self and your hearers (1 Timothy 4:12-16).

When you infiltrate, there's a good chance that someone older won't
like that someone younger is trying to influence them—even if it's with
commitment to Jesus. *What's this kid got to say to me? I've been a Christian twice as long as he has,* they think.

Channel reactions like this into a deeper longing to know God
more, to know his Word more, and to walk like Jesus more. Fact is,
we've all got a ton of pride. And just as it's not the easiest thing to
be looked down on, it's also not the easiest thing to have someone
younger than you shedding light on a dark area in your life—especially spiritually.

To choose a lifestyle of infiltration is a scary thing. And sometimes,
you're going to fail. You're going to say something or do something that

doesn't have biblical support or is contrary to what Jesus taught. And someone will call you out on it.

This is a good thing. Iron sharpening iron. It may hurt your pride—mine has taken its share of lashes—but it's a mercy of God when you get corrected and gain a broader perspective about what it means to follow Jesus. The key is to joyfully learn and never give up in your desire to be like Christ.

> When we hold our rights and privileges too tightly and refuse to let anyone take advantage of us, when we resist opening ourselves up to being hurt or disappointed—under any circumstances—we do not live as one who's on the receiving end of God's grace.[12]
>
> Ed Stetzer

Infiltration requires a deep trust in yourself. Not because of who you are, but because of who lives in you. Difficult situations and depressing feelings will come when you infiltrate. When they do, you must know that age doesn't matter. It's Jesus inside you that matters.

So don't worry when your infiltrating isn't going as you envisioned. Don't crawl into a corner after you've failed. Failure happens. Expect it. Move on.

CHAPTER 8

How to Infiltrate
—Two

Become an Amateur Profiler

> Do your best to present yourself to God as one approved,
> a worker who has no need to be ashamed, rightly han-
> dling the word of truth. But avoid irreverent babble, for it
> will lead people into more and more ungodliness...Have
> nothing to do with foolish, ignorant controversies; you
> know that they breed quarrels. And the Lord's servant must
> not be quarrelsome but kind to everyone, able to teach,
> patiently enduring evil, correcting his opponents with gen-
> tleness. God may perhaps grant them repentance leading
> to a knowledge of the truth (2 Timothy 2:15-16,23-25).

I fidgeted by number 2's locker, hoping that the captain, Derek
Jeter, would arrive before I lost courage.

The New York Yankees had won and all of the reporters were fin-
ishing interviews in the Yankee clubhouse. A couple of them thanked
Mariano Rivera for his time, and a scattered few did the same around
Jorge Posada and Roger Clemens. The clubhouse door closed and I
knew I was the last reporter standing amid the lockers of legends. I
prayed security wouldn't shuffle me out.

"How's it going, buddy?" Jeter said, walking out of the trainer's
room with his never-changing calmness.

Just like all of my friends, I had loved hating the Yankees. I had always badmouthed "pretty-boy" Jeter and thought of him as cocky and arrogant.

After spending a season covering him, I knew I'd gotten him *way* wrong.

And what I did next was my way of saying just that.

"I...just finished reading your book," I said.

"Oh yeah?" He grabbed his jacket from his locker, and I immediately felt like I should go. He had people to see, a city to own. But there was something about his eyes. He wasn't telling me to go.

"It meant a lot," I said. "Everything you said about chasing your dream and doing the right thing."

"Thank you, man—really appreciate that," Jeter said.

To know someone accurately, you have to talk with him, observe him, and ask questions of him.

We need to do this in our churches.

The moment you decide to infiltrate is the moment you must add "amateur profiler" to your résumé. Because infiltration takes constant profiling.

Profiling probably isn't the most liked term in the world, so let me clarify. The profiling I'm advocating for isn't the kind that arrogantly believes it knows everything about another person just because of the clothes they wear or how they talk.

The profiling I'm advocating for is about humbly getting to know your brothers' and sisters' tendencies in four areas of the Christian life: love, trust, obedience, and knowledge. It's about entering conversations intentionally attuned to how they're presenting their spiritual state.

How Amateur Profiling Works

The most important part of profiling is paying attention.

For example, when a brother or sister expresses their trust in Jesus through their words or actions, mentally filter it into the "trust" canister, as shown in the chart below. When they express their obedience to Jesus in some way, filter it into the "obedience" canister. And so forth.

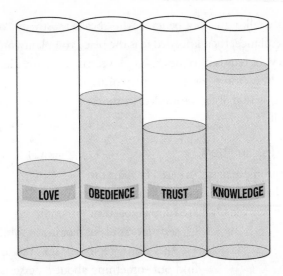

Through this process, you don't necessarily learn what your brother or sister is lacking spiritually. You simply discover what they emphasize, which equips you with everything you need as an Infiltrator.

You don't always remember the little snippets you filter and store away. But your subconscious mind is so powerful that it doesn't matter. If you put any effort at all into trying to understand someone's pattern in terms of love, trust, obedience, and knowledge, your brain works one hundred times harder than you do and it won't leave you blank when you're trying to remember.

As soon as a pattern emerges you are ready to, like Paul, "become all things to all people" and bring focus to your infiltration (1 Corinthians 9:19-23). Becoming all things is simply meeting people where they're most comfortable. Paul witnessed differently to different people groups. He found a connection point within the context of the culture, started there, then moved the conversation to the truth about salvation.

Pinpointing patterns of love, trust, obedience, and knowledge allows you to operate in the same way.

When the majority of what your brother or sister says or does fills the love canister, or the obedience canister, or perhaps a combination of both, then you have a safe foundation from which to reach into the unexplored spiritual territory in their lives.

If you're talking with a believer who speaks mostly out of knowledge, for instance, then knowledge is the place you plant your foot as you reach your hands into the areas of love, trust, and obedience.

We're always more comfortable exploring something new if we're grounded in something familiar.

> Jesus' words to people in need were not all the same...The reality is "one size fits all" does not work.[1]
>
> Ed Stetzer

Things to Remember

Never profile in haste. Instead of relying on your gut, have three long conversations with your fellow believer. Or share a dinner together.

> God will ask each member of the body..."Did you treat the weaker parts as indispensable, and did you treat the parts that most think less honorable with special honor?"[2]
>
> Mark Dever

Or serve alongside him or her in some way.

And don't get hung up. Too often we find out something about a person, such as their political affiliation or stance on a cultural hot topic, and we immediately grow cold to them. This usually leads to all kinds of wrong assumptions and sinful behavior. Instead, aspire to know these believers at an even deeper level. If we are ever to sharpen each other as one sword sharpens another, we need to be willing to step into the minds of others, think as they do, and then use what we've learned to push both them and ourselves toward deeper commitment to Jesus.

How to Build Bridges

Knowing someone's pattern makes it possible for you to infiltrate in a way that is safe to your fellow believers. The next step of the Infiltrator is to build bridges from that area of safety to the areas of less comfort. Because the areas of less comfort are what hold believers back from the abundant life of total, passionate commitment to Jesus.

> God has willed that we should seek and find His living Word in the witness of a brother, in the mouth of man. Therefore, the Christian needs another Christian who speaks God's Word to him.[3]
>
> Dietrich Bonhoeffer

What you'll read next is a lot to think about, so I want to take a moment to clarify the main point. The following bridges aren't meant to be a step-by-step guide you put into motion as you infiltrate. They're simply practical ideas and strategies for your subconscious to store away as spontaneous opportunities arise. Trust God to serve them to your tongue when the real thing happens.

To build a bridge from knowledge, zero in on the theology in Scripture that points to love, trust, and obedience.

From Knowledge to Love

We know from the Bible that the greatest commandment is to love God with all of our heart, soul, and mind—and to love our neighbors as ourselves. From this, the Infiltrator can continually bring the conversation back to the fact that God wants our heart and soul, not just our mind.

A great question to explore when moving from knowledge to love is, *What does it mean to love God with your heart and soul?* But it's imperative that you continually hit the fact that God puts this commandment above all others. Without this emphasis, words like *heart* and *soul* breeze past the person of knowledge. You need to shock them alive to love by focusing on God's commandment of it.

From Knowledge to Obedience

Knowledge that doesn't inform our actions is dead. Knowing that God is real is not the same as obeying him. Even the demons believe, and shudder (James 2:19). The Pharisees, for whom Jesus reserved his harshest words, were filled with knowledge of Scripture—but it didn't translate into obedience to the Son.

A great question to explore when moving from knowledge to obedience is deadness. But just like love, there must be a supplementary emphasis. The idea of deadness tends to go in one ear and out the other of a knowledge believer, because the knowledge believer's mental filter informs him or her that they know about deadness—and therefore are obviously not dead. In other words, knowledge equals accuracy and rightness. So it's important to emphasize the idea that the dead don't know they're dead, and that many dead people who think they're alive will one day cry out to Jesus in vain (Matthew 7:21-23).

From Knowledge to Trust

The Bible has plenty of things to say about trust. Proverbs 3:5 says, "Trust in the LORD with all your heart, and do not lean on your own understanding." This is a great verse to start the connection from knowledge to trust. The knowledge believer usually believes that knowledge of trust is the same as trust. So you need to help show knowledge believers that trust is very active, and that when we truly trust God, we live differently.

> Knowing about God and knowing Him personally are galaxies apart. Recognize the difference and choose well. That one decision will make all the difference.[4]
>
> Wayne Cordeiro

A great place of discussion is Hebrews 11, which shows us that active trust in God makes us speak boldly as we should, go where he leads us to go, follow God in ways that are unthinkable to us, and take part in things that should otherwise be impossible. This makes for a great contrast to the comfort-first, warranty-labeled, always-insured society that knowledge believers tend to buy into. It opens the discussion of what active trust must look like in a believer's life today.

To build a bridge from love, zero in on the emotional aspects of Scripture that point toward our need for obedience, trust, and knowledge.

From Love to Obedience

The Bible is filled with beautiful, emotional outpouring of love and worship to God. God is love, we read in 1 John 4:7, and everyone who loves is born of God. This is a great place to start. It establishes and affirms the love-filled believer's passionate longing for God.

From that point, the most powerful place to connect love to obedience is through the most beautiful picture of love, Jesus, who, though he was affectionate with his followers, didn't choose to emphasize affection as the way to show our love to him. He chose obedience, saying,

"If you love me, you will keep my commandments" (John 14:15). This opens the door to talk about all of the imperative commands in the Bible about knowing God, trusting in him, and obeying him (many of which are found in "The Follower Manifesto" in chapter 4).

From Love to Trust

Love and trust are deeply connected. We just don't always see it until someone we love does not trust us. To move the love believer to trust, it's important to make this connection visible to them.

A few years ago I felt called to do something but was unwilling because the risk was too great. I felt so convicted that I had to get out of the house, take a drive, and talk with God. And during that drive, I recalled how I longed for someone I loved to trust that I could do something despite horrible odds. But the trust wasn't there, and it tore my heart. In that moment, I realized that I was tearing God's heart in the same way by not following his leading. He wanted me to trust him in spite of horrible odds.

So I drove home, trusted, and the course of my life drastically changed because of it. God showed me that loving him was one thing, but that trusting him was another. I needed to believe that he who takes care of birds and animals would take care of me, his child, so much more. I needed to trust that he who says he will never leave me or forsake me never *will*. I needed to trust that *all* things are possible through him.

Think of these things when helping a love believer move toward trust in Christ.

From Love to Knowledge

Similar to above, pointing to the greatest commandment is a great start in helping the love believer move toward knowledge. The words "loving God with all of your heart and soul" leap off the page so much to the love believer that the "mind" part can pass by unnoticeably. So here, the Infiltrator needs to shine a spotlight on the idea of loving God with our mind and what that means in day-to-day life.

Great bridging verses for this are those that deal with growing in knowledge (2 Peter 3:18), maturing (1 Corinthians 14:20), and loving God's Word (Psalm 119:97-104).

To build a bridge from trust, zero in on the faith elements of Scripture that point to love, obedience, and knowledge.

From Trust to Love

A great starting point for the trust believer is the father-child relationship we have with God. As we saw in chapter 6, "What Comes Next," childlikeness is the essence of trust. But we know that children don't just trust their father. They love him. They want to be close to him and sit on his lap.

Emphasize these things when infiltrating the trust believer. If the trust believer you're focusing on never knew his or her father, or has a rough history there, speak of someone he or she admired as a kid.

From Trust to Obedience

The trust believer is so full of faith in God that, sometimes, they do not fully realize the ramifications of whom or what they're putting their trust into. They trust that the Bible is right and true but might not ever read God's Word. They trust that God is powerful and can do anything but might not ever pray or expect him to do anything extraordinary.

Trust can be little more than belief that God is real—and, as noted above, that isn't any more than the demons believe. As you infiltrate the trust believer, spend a good amount of time in verses that talk about the Word of God as trustworthy (2 Timothy 3:16). From there, point to passages about obedience and reiterate that true trust is proven by how our lives reflect our trust. Make special note of the parable of the two sons, where we see that doing is more important than saying (Matthew 21:28-32).

From Trust to Knowledge

Similar to obedience, the key here is to understand that, just as faith without works is dead, trust without knowledge ignores the wonderful blessings God has given us to know him better. Such as reading his Word and discovering his incredible attributes and three-in-one personhood.

To help move the trust believer to knowledge, ask him or her about the people they trust most. From there, dig deeper. Ask them why these people deserve trust. Help him or her see that putting trust in God with no real desire of wanting to know him just doesn't fit. Because the people we trust are the people we know best.

To build a bridge from obedience, you must zero in on the commands of Scripture that point to love, trust, and knowledge.

From Obedience to Love

Along with using the greatest commandment as a starting point, it's good to point the obedience believer to commandments in Scripture about worship and childlikeness. Both are filled with great pictures of love that help put a face to loving "God with all of your heart."

From Obedience to Trust

This can be really difficult for the obedience believer, because the idea of trust has very little skin to it. It's hard to visualize. So start with the fact that it's impossible to please God without faith (Hebrews 11:6). This is rattling to the obedience believer, who desperately wants to please him through what they do outwardly.

As you infiltrate, focus on the idea of the unseen obedience that God requires more than anything: the obedience of the heart—that is, trust.

From Obedience to Knowledge

When helping an obedience believer in the realm of knowledge, consider the story of Uzzah in 2 Samuel 6:1-8. Uzzah tried to obey God according to his own standards—not according to what God had said. Instead of obeying the command to not touch the Ark, Uzzah made a split-second decision assuming God would be pleased if he kept the Ark from falling into mud.

On that fateful day, Uzzah died because he followed his own way instead of obeying what he knew God had said.

Use Sin Subtlety

> Let your speech always be gracious, seasoned with salt, so that you may know how you ought to answer each person (Colossians 4:6).

Sin subtlety is about using your own sin and struggles to help others see some of their sin and struggles.

To employ sin subtlety is to, when opportunity arises, specifically speak from your own marred background that has to do with 1) your church's greatest lacking or 2) an individual's greatest lacking.

> I wonder how we as a church think we are ever going to be very good at evangelism or world missions if we are not very good at applying the gospel of Christ to our own hearts and to the relationships we have right in our own churches.[5]
>
> Mark Dever

Have you ever struggled with devaluing a certain personality type? Logical people, maybe? Or perhaps creative types? Does your church struggle in the same way? Use your background as a launch pad to speak up about God's intricate and unique design of every person on earth. Point conversations to being fearfully and wonderfully made, showing that God does not love a creative or logical person any less than the other.

Even though you try, is it hard for you to tell others about Jesus? Is it a weakness in your church as well? Speak up from your struggle. Humbly point to the great commission and how much emphasis Jesus puts on sharing his love and truth to every soul on earth. Provoke others to think, weep, and change with you.

In what ways has your walk with Jesus become lukewarm? Have you grown numb in any way? What about your church? Speak up about your numbness. Talk about how we as the body fall into the trap of just showing up on Sunday, looking good, and saying the right things. Direct conversations toward the Pharisees and Jesus's harshness with those who worried about how they looked on the outside while neglecting what was going on in the inside (Luke 11:39).

Is worship just another part of being a Christian to you? Have you ever lost the wonder of truly praising the God of the universe? What about the people in your church? Are they the same? Speak up about your desire to always walk away from worship with a sense of awe, wonder, and thankfulness. Talk about worshipping from the heart instead of just paying lip service (Isaiah 29:13). Focus on how people who experienced God in the Bible were utterly changed by their encounters.

> Enduring the wounds of fellow Christians with mercy and grace seems to be the call of every true saint. We should not expect it to be any different in our own lives.[6]
>
> Stephen Mansfield

Do you have a hard time understanding the depths and intricacies of the Bible? The doctrines and theology? Has this ever made you ignore parts of Scripture? Does your church ever ignore parts of Scripture? Speak up about the full knowledge of God and how he isn't pleased when neglect parts of his Word.

Obviously, it's not smart to come off as the Bible police. Without humility and subtlety, doing any of these is pointless.

Below are some ways to humbly go about subtlety.

Share Stories

There is great power in sharing your stories of God's work in your life. Just think about the best stories you've ever heard and how they've stuck in your mind. They make their homes in the back of your brain and come to life whenever the opportunity arises to share them.

> Being a kingdom agent means becoming one who "loses his life" from a worldly point of view (Mark 8:35) in order to find true life for ourselves and to help rescue others who are chained in darkness, doubt, and cleverly disguised despair.[7]
>
> Ed Stetzer

Stories are a powerful way to employ sin subtlety. Think about how Jesus taught through parables—even when the people depicted in his parables were standing right in front of him. Stories are a great way of saying something loudly without having to say it loudly.

Bring Up Something You Read

This is another great reason to read broadly. Bringing up something you read that speaks directly into where your church or an individual is lacking is more subtle than quoting a verse. It's a way to ease into conversations and open the door for the Scripture to flow naturally when your brother or sister is more receptive.

Seize the Moment

When someone says or does something that, even in the littlest way, shows forward movement in the area they're most lacking, jump on it. Praise your brother or sister for it. Not in a way that draws attention. Just a simple, "Hey, I noticed when you said or did _____. That's been on my heart and really spoke to me. Thank you."

Bring in Others to Ease Tension

Sometimes believers get very uncomfortable about subjects no matter how subtle you are. They feel attacked or belittled. One way to preempt this is to bring others into the conversation so that the timid believer with you can hear what he or she needs to hear, but in a way that's safe. Larger group discussions bring in more iron to sharpen iron as well, which is a nice bonus.

Subject-Jump

It's hard to infiltrate when no one is anywhere close to the subject you're seeking to bring up. When you find yourself in this position, try subject-jumping through word-association. Someone might be talking up football, for instance, and you can mention a Christian player. From there, you most likely can find a way to direct the conversation into things about faith.

> Going away is easy... Humble yourself and acknowledge that you need other Christians. Invite them into your life. Stop complaining about what's wrong with the church, and become part of a solution.[8]
>
> Joshua Harris

How to Get into Conversations

The hardest part about infiltrating is starting. Because starting is kind of like stepping up to the plate after spending a bunch of time reading about how to hit. The two aren't entirely foreign to each other, but they're just so different. In reading about how to hit, you have organized information. In stepping to the plate, you have chaotic decision making.

Let's say you've gone to church, worshipped God, and listened to the sermon. The moment the service is over is the perfect segue into infiltration. You've poured into God and his shepherd has poured his Word into you. Now all that's left is pouring into the person next to you.

> Start where you are. Use what you have. Do what you can.[9]
>
> Ed Stetzer

To get into a conversation with another believer is as simple as saying good morning. From there, it's just a matter of intentionally moving the conversation toward questions that ignite infiltration, such as:

- What did the sermon stir inside you?
- How have you seen God this week?
- What are you praying about these days?
- What has God been teaching you?

These questions are pretty much the only thing scripted in the process. Because, just like hitting a baseball, infiltration is all about split-second reactions and hitting the ball where it's pitched.

> Your church will be no more involved than you are involved. She will be no more devoted than you are. No more genuine than you are. No more positive than you are.[10]
>
> Wayne Cordeiro

That said, sometimes you get into a conversation and ask good questions, but it just isn't a two-way street. The other person is guarded, shy, or just disinterested.

At that point it's important to change your approach from asking questions to telling stories. Your stories. Not just for the sake of filling the air. But with intentionality. With the purpose of gently coaxing the person out of whatever is keeping them locked up. Sometimes people just need you to go first where you're asking them to go.

If that doesn't open up the conversation, then bring up something you read or watched recently, or call someone else into the conversation, or ask them how you can pray for them. This opens the door for you to take them before God in prayer with some specifics, and also makes for a great conversation starter the next time you see him or her.

The whole thing may or may not feel a little awkward or unsettling, but sometimes, this is the way of infiltration. And the more times you do it, the less awkward and unsettling it becomes.

Practice Tone-Setting

Every church has a tone, a feel that leans toward love, trust, obedience, knowledge, or some combination of these. Infiltrating through tone-setting focuses on infusing the glue of unity, depth, and purpose into whatever makeup your church has.

> If you can work on yourself, then as you interact with others, the church will change. In short, if you do the hard work of allowing God to change you, the whole system will change.[11]
>
> Peter Scazzero

Here are ways to tone-set these three kinds of glue in your church.

Tone-Set Unity

> So if there is any encouragement in Christ, any comfort from love, any participation in the Spirit, any affection and sympathy, complete my joy by being of the same mind, having the same love, being in full accord and of one mind (Philippians 2:1-2).

It's been said that if you want to know what's really important to someone, pay attention to what they talk about in their final days on earth.

Jesus talked about unity.

> When we join our lives with honest relationships, we can better provoke one another to love and good deeds.[12]
>
> Ed Stetzer

On the night before he died, he prayed, "I do not ask for these [disciples] only, but also for those who will believe in me through their word, that they may all be one, just as you, Father, are in me, and I in you, that they also may be in us, so that the world may believe that you have sent me" (John 17:20-21).

Jesus prayed that all believers, existing and future, would be united. That we would get along and accept each other's weirdness and differences—all for the reason that the world would know that God, his Son, and their love are real.

> Let us work for unity in belief and peace in our churches, remembering that "it is an honor for a man to keep aloof from strife, but every fool will be quarreling." [13]
>
> Thabiti M. Anyabwile

Our unity is like one of the wonders of the world: It stands out. It's what makes the world crane its neck and take notice. What glues these people together? What gives them joy? What compels them to love?

Unity is of utmost importance to Jesus, and it needs to be to us as well. Below are three ways to tone-set unity in the body of Christ.

1. Learn First Names

One of the easiest ways of creating unity in church is to learn first names and call other believers "brother" and "sister"—especially if this isn't common in your church. Doing so stirs up the sense that, yes, we truly are family. We are connected by something thicker than human blood. We are bonded in Christ, and it's an excellent thing when our lives reflect that.

2. Promote Unity, Not Uniformity

Sometimes churches get caught in a rut of everyone looking and sounding the same. Do what you can to promote the opposite of that. Either be different yourself, or encourage others who are different. Make it a point of showing other believers that unity isn't about our externals, but our internal purpose of commitment to Jesus.

> The Bible calls us as a family to be connected to one another in relationship in such a loving way that the world will know that Jesus is real and alive. [14]
>
> Peter Scazzero

There came a point in my church life when I recognized that everyone looked very much alike—myself included. When I visualized myself as a newcomer to our church, I came to the conclusion that they would feel highly obligated to look like the church's mold. This wasn't healthy. We needed people to walk into our church feeling as though what they looked like on the outside didn't matter.

So I purposely started looking different. I wanted to be the one a newcomer would remember and think, "If the church accepts him, maybe it would accept me too." I know that sounds a little prideful, but it's really just being intentional.

3. Speak Well of Other Churches and Believers

Judging others is a problem in the church. And not just judging others who don't know Jesus, but those who do. Make it a point to speak well of other churches and denominations that love Jesus. And when others in your church don't, be the first to speak up for the sake of unity.

Always point believers to the fact that we are many people, in many churches, with many pastors, under one head: Jesus Christ. He is the leader. He is the judge. He is the only one who can gaze into our motives. So we shouldn't live as though that's our role. We shouldn't put other churches down just because they're different.

Instead we should celebrate the love, trust, obedience, and knowledge that they excel in.

> He who looks upon his brother should know that he will be eternally united with him in Jesus Christ.[15]
>
> Dietrich Bonhoeffer

> As much as God accomplishes through our outward-focused efforts and ministries, he can do amazing things just through the visible interactivity of God's people living our sold-out lives together, day in and day out for our King.[16]
>
> Ed Stetzer

> Human love can never understand spiritual love, for spiritual love is from above; it is something completely strange, new, and incomprehensible to all earthly love.[17]
>
> Dietrich Bonhoeffer

Tone-Set Depth

For wisdom will enter your heart, and knowledge will be pleasant to your soul; discretion will watch over you, understanding will guard you (Proverbs 2:10-11).

Depth refuses to settle for shallowness in any part of the Christian life.

Depth helps us understand the difficult things in life and Scripture. Depth helps us take seriously the hard commandments Jesus calls us to.

> We must reject easy answers to life's hardest questions. We must admit that such questions are hard to reconcile with the tensions we know. To live the Jesus life well means we will have to jettison easy answers and pious platitudes.[18]
>
> Stephen W. Smith

When depth looks at an apparent paradox—faith and works, sovereignty and responsibility, love and wrath—it doesn't question the authority of God as though he's made some cosmic blunder. It wonders at the complexity of his mind and power.

Depth isn't about being smarter or more intricate than everyone else. It's about practicing the way of love, trust, obedience, and knowledge to the best of your ability so that you can help others live out the uncomplicated gospel of loving God, loving others, doing justice, and walking humbly.

In other words, depth is about helping others live totally committed to Jesus.

Below are three ways to tone-set depth in the body of Christ.

1. Create Opportunities for Conversations and Ask Good Questions

In order to tone-set depth, you need to get to know people's beliefs, values, goals, and desires. You need to identify with people in their unique stages of maturity in Christ, accept them where they are, and build them up from there.

> The first service that one owes to others in the fellowship consists in listening to them. Just as love to God begins with listening to his Word, so the beginning of love for the brethren is learning to listen to them.[19]
>
> Dietrich Bonhoeffer

Much of this comes in the form of conversation. But this takes effort. You must seek it out. You need to plan. You need to set your mind on messaging someone, or approaching him or her at church, or simply clearing dates on your calendar for spontaneity.

Most importantly, once you get together you need to ask good questions. Because without good questions, conversation goes to effortless topics: the weather, sports, and other top-of-the-mind things.

I like to do something my friend and author Jim Rubart calls "ask, listen." It's a powerful concept he teaches that can be boiled down like this: First, ask people about their lives. Not just their regular lives (job, school, relationships), but also their spiritual lives (relationship with God, what God is teaching them, how God is working, how their heart is). Then listen. Nod. Encourage them to keep going. Do everything you can to give them permission to be real with you. If courtesy answers are given—short answers that deflect the talking back to you—then push a little bit. Keep the spotlight on the person you're talking with.

Rubart also talks about remembering.

Remember what people tell you. Make their burdens your burdens. Make their hurts your hurts. Take ownership in their lives by remembering their successes and failures. When you remember, your mind forms a file on that person. And the next time you enter a conversation, you reopen the file and start adding more. As the files build, so does the mutual trust between you and your fellow brother or sister you're infiltrating. You start sharing a deeper connection.

> I often heard only part of what was said, framing my reply rather than entering their world. Like many others, I was often too busy contradicting, correcting, judging, or rebutting to really understand what other people meant or were feeling.[20]
>
> Peter Scazzero

This is true fellowship. This is how you open doors to stir others to greater commitment.

2. Bring Your Voice to the Table

When I was young, I didn't think I could add value in my church's classes or small groups. I was a kid. I didn't know the Bible like the others did. I was there to soak up, and that's it.

I wish I could have some of those years back. Because now I see the value in saying what's on your mind and asking good questions. If you constantly bring these two facets to the table, you add great value to everyone else. Not because your words are more important. But because the more perspectives and questions there are, the closer everyone gets to the truth.

Seize every opportunity you have when talking about your faith with other believers. Say what's on your heart. Ask good questions. Add value.

3. Be Berean

The Bereans in Acts examined everything they heard others say about God, and tested it for accuracy. We need to be like them. We need to own our knowledge and understanding of the Bible, study deeply, and confront those who present Scripture for anything less than what it is.

The Bereans weren't some stuck up, everything-you-say-about-the-Bible-is-wrong kind of people. They "received the word with all eagerness," and were made of noble character (Acts 17:11). They tested for truth not to be right, but to honor God.

When we are not Berean, we tend to soak up whatever we hear and think of it as fact, when in reality it might be a half-truth or just plain false. Don't be a believer who counts on your pastor alone for biblical depth and knowledge. Make it your responsibility.

Proverbs 17:17 says, "The one who states his case first seems right, until the other comes and examines him."

Be that examiner. Be Berean.

Serve Another Church

Unity is greatly lacking in church. We desperately need to pull together as the body of Christ and work together for the purpose of Christ. But too often our denominational differences and lack of interest in collaborating keep us from helping each other pull together. We must choose to cross bridges and lines, and we must do this by placing the responsibility on us.

This brings us to serving other churches.

- Try going to other churches and leaving encouraging notes for pastors (or write them an email).

- Call up a church and ask what kind of events they have coming up, and then offer to set up before the event, take down afterward, bring food or water, pray for the event, or run unforeseen errands.

- Create one big childcare facility at your church for a night, so that another church can be freed to do ministry or just take a night off to rejuvenate as a body. You can go work on the grounds of another church, or find other ways to free others of their normal duties.

I know it can feel like you're not fulfilling the great commission when you're doing behind-the-scenes work, but God is pleased when we're focused on his work, whether we're on the front lines or the back.

Create a Feeder Table

Back when I was a sports reporter, I used to write about annual "feeder" games. These games were put together to showcase the top talent around the league so that coaches could pick and choose their all-star squads.

In a similar sense, creating feeder conversations can lead to all-star quality conversations in homes. This is how it works.

> Telling your story is one of the best ways to be known and create a sense of community. While there is definitely a time and place to open the Bible and study it, we can often hide behind the study and never really get to know each other.[21]
>
> Stephen W. Smith

1. First, decide on a certain day of the month or week that you'd like to meet. Don't make it so often that it becomes burdensome. Just make it enough to where people look forward to coming.

2. Second, find a gifted moderator and facilitator. Many churches organize groups like this, but they fail because of a lack of leading. When there isn't a solid facilitator,

someone will dominate the conversation, set the wrong tone, or utterly suck the group of its power. The facilitator must lay ground rules quickly and stick to them. He or she must be in tune with what weakens the time together and always aim to build up the group.

3. Third, keep the atmosphere informal and organic. This stirs up authenticity and helps others get real about their lives, creating room for infiltration.

Tone-Set Purpose

I have been crucified with Christ. It is no longer I who live, but Christ who lives in me. And the life I now live in the flesh I live by faith in the Son of God, who loved me and gave himself for me (Galatians 2:20).

Infiltrators tone-set purpose by speaking often of their life's mission: to radically love God, love people, do justice, love mercy, and walk humbly—all because of Jesus.

Tone-setting purpose is about helping others in church to see that the body of Christ is so much more than a place where believers meet.

> People are moved toward God because of the vision for a higher purpose than mere assembly.[22]
>
> Ed Stetzer

It's about being a constant glow of head-over-heels passion and commitment to Jesus for all that he is and all that he's done. It's about speaking of heaven because we anticipate it. And it's about getting amped up about living with abandoned love and showing through our lives that *God is real.*

Honestly…how can we not? If Christ lives in us, then our lives will reflect his great purpose.

1. Speak As Though Jesus Lives

Jesus is the reason we are fully alive. And one of the best ways to tone-set purpose is to talk as though he lives. *Really* lives.

If Jesus didn't die on the cross and rise from the dead, then

Christianity is pointless. The sad part about this is that many in church today do not speak, verbally or emotionally, that Jesus lives. So Christianity comes off as kind of pointless.

Tone-setting purpose starts with talking about Jesus, and how he died for you, how he saved you, and what he's commanded of you. When you continually gush about Jesus, other believers can't help but think—*Oh yeah, that's what it's supposed to be about...*

> What a difficult thing it often is to utter the name of Jesus Christ in the presence even of a brother![23]
>
> Dietrich Bonhoeffer

Tone-setting purpose through your love for Christ does wonders in stirring up the Spirit in others who are going through the motions.

When tone-setting purpose, start with Jesus.

2. Discover and Use Your Gifts

> For as in one body we have many members, and the members do not all have the same function, so we, though many, are one body in Christ, and individually members one of another. Having gifts that differ according to the grace given to us, let us use them (Romans 12:4-6).

Finding your passion and using your gifts for Jesus radiates that your belief isn't merely belief. It's belief that's grounded. Belief that translates into where you put your time and money.

To radiate purpose, you need to discover how God has gifted you and use those gifts to serve him. Serving the body of Christ with your gifts demonstrates to others that you're invested.

You can't fake spiritual gifts. You can't fake passion. You can't fake giving God everything you have for his kingdom. And when something cannot be faked, people know it's real.

> I often hear Christians talking about their different spiritual gifts. Yet I wonder how often people consider the fact that God has given so many gifts precisely so that those gifts might be used in response to the sin of other Christians in the church.[24]
>
> Mark Dever

3. Make Peace Your Goal

> If possible, so far as it depends on you, live peaceably with all (Romans 12:18).

When you make peace your goal, people notice.

Peace requires forgiveness. Peace requires grace. Peace requires overlooking offenses. All of these require supernatural help from God because they do not come naturally to us. And people notice the supernatural. It points to something bigger.

> The stories of wounding and offense could fill a thousand books and still be unfinished…If Christianity teaches anything, it is that men are deeply flawed and need rescue.[25]
>
> Stephen Mansfield

Receive what others say with grace, have a teachable spirit, refuse to argue, gossip, or get the last word, speak with love and respect, and pray for those who are hostile to you.

Use Social Media

> Show yourself in all respects to be a model of good works, and in your teaching show integrity, dignity, and sound speech that cannot be condemned, so that an opponent may be put to shame, having nothing evil to say about us (Titus 2:7-8).

We're always using social media. Our lives are an open book. We're constantly writing statuses, responding to comments, sending and receiving messages, liking posts, and, if you're a creeper, poking people.

That carries a lot of influence. It opens great opportunities for infiltration. You can:

- Discuss aspects of your walk with Jesus
- Be bold when others are shy
- Be authentic and real and subtly encourage others to do the same

Every piece of content you write is valuable. Social media opens the door for your brothers and sisters to see what's going on in your spiritual life. They know where you stand whether or not they engage with what you post. And this, in a small way, contributes to infiltration.

Leave the Results to God

> And we know that for those who love God all things work together for good, for those who are called according to his purpose (Romans 8:28).

Results are not the objective of the Infiltrator. Consistency is.

If it seems like nothing is working out as you infiltrate, that doesn't mean it's not doing any good or that God didn't call you to it. It means that he's working all things for good, even if it's mysterious and unsearchable. It's impossible to know how God is working. But it is completely possible to trust that he's working.

A year ago my sister-in-law found herself living alone after her family moved out of state. She applied for jobs in a bad job market, plummeted into more and more debt, and didn't get the dream job she had applied for—or any of her secondary options. The immediate future was bleak for her.

The night she hit an all-time low, my wife and I knew we needed to do something, so we checked our finances. But God had something better. A few days later, my sister-in-law got a call and was offered the dream job she'd previously missed out on.

> It is God himself who makes the plea through us, his fellow workers, and his Spirit who guarantees that his Word will not return void. We are to plant and water faithfully, confidently trusting that God will give the increase.[26]
>
> Thabiti M. Anyabwile

What was God up to during that process? What was he teaching? We just don't know. All we know is that under the surface, everything just might be going right.

So as you infiltrate, don't focus on the results. Focus on doing what you can do—nothing more, nothing less.

What Now?

Watch this chapter's video at www.calledtostay.com.

Get the download of the "Evaluate Your Church" test here: www .calledtostay.com.

"Today I infiltrated by…" — Post this as your Facebook status and I'll join the conversation (just remember to tag me).

Start asking your brothers and sisters, "How's your heart?" You won't believe how quickly this simple question cuts straight to the soul.

What's Next

Everything up to this point has been about why you should stay in church and how to stay in a way that adds incredible value to the body of Christ. The next chapter is the direct opposite.

We're going to talk about when it's time to leave.

PART 3

Age of the Infiltrator

CHAPTER 9

When to Leave

Infiltrating Is Not for Everyone

> And if anyone will not receive you or listen to your words,
> shake off the dust from your feet when you leave that house
> or town (Matthew 10:14).

Devin used to go to a church where only seminary-educated folks were allowed to have an opinion. Audrey's church treated her like an unbeliever for asking questions about the Bible. Camille received a tithe card six months after leaving her church.

William's congregation avoided him because his tattoos and clothing didn't fit in. Chad's church raked him for taking medication and seeking professional help outside of the church. Torrey got shunned for seeking guidance about her sexuality. And Jason's church stalked him online then blasted him for things that weren't even wrong.

If a producer decided to make a horror film about the church, he'd start with stories like these.

In this chapter, I want to explore how to discover when you should leave a church, change churches, and also how to talk with your pastors.

If you're a believer, God has put his Holy Spirit inside you. He's also given you a direct connection to him through prayer and his Word. These work together in how he reveals what he wants us to do. But we also abuse them. When it comes to finding God's will, too often we convince ourselves that we're hearing what sounds good to us. So before we move into hearing from God, consider his will for us: To respect our pastors and leaders, be at peace with others, admonish the idle, encourage the fainthearted, help the weak, be patient with all, seek to do good to believers and nonbelievers alike, and to rejoice always and pray without ceasing, giving thanks in all circumstances (1 Thessalonians 5:12-19).

> We should pray for our leaders' boldness, clarity, and consistency with the gospel message, and for the opportunity for them to proclaim Christ.[1]
>
> Thabiti M. Anyabwile

As we dive into when you should leave, don't lose focus of what God has said here.

Pray, Read, Feel

Before you make your decision to leave or stay, you must pray fervently, meditate on God's Word, and stand ready for the Spirit's guiding.

- Pray: Get on your knees before God. Shut out the world. Tell him what he means to you, and that you want to obey him in everything. Express what's on your heart. Ask him what he wants you to do, and for the strength to do it. And ask him to expose the parts of yourself that even you don't know about. Ask him to make your motives pure.

- Read: God speaks through his Word. Don't neglect it. Immerse yourself in what he says. Not just verse by verse, but entire books of the Bible. Ask that you would hear his truth clearly. Talk with other believers you respect and get their advice.

- Feel: We need to stand ready for how God moves inside us. How are you convicted? Do you feel peace or anxiety about leaving your church? Are you hearing what God wants you to hear, or just what sounds good? Ask him to let clarity and peace guide you.

Although only you can conclude God's path for you, there are definitely questions and prompts that can help.

Here are some reasons for why you should consider leaving, what to consider before leaving, and advice for moving on.

When to Consider Leaving

Consider leaving your church if:

- You're throwing pearls before swine.
- It's destroying you or your family.
- You're not allowed to think differently from the pastor.
- You're being abused.
- You're receiving threats that you're not a Christian anymore.
- Leadership falls into sin and refuses to repent.
- Your pastor doesn't use the Bible as his final authority.
- The Spirit is clearly moving you to leave.

> We are called to be committed to the church. But sometimes that commitment involves leaving an unbiblical church.[2]
>
> Joshua Harris

What to Consider Before Leaving

Ask yourself:

- Am I leaving in the heat of the moment?
- Have I done all I can do, or am I a part of the problem?
- Am I leaving over trite details in light of what Jesus has done for me?
- Have I loved the people I'm leaving or walked a mile in their shoes?
- Am I praying for those who've hurt me?
- Is my anger righteous or just bitter?
- Am I slandering those who've hurt me?
- Am I feeling spiritually elite in any way?

- Have I confessed my sins to God and others?
- Have I sought the advice from those I respect?
- Is God calling me to infiltrate?

Talking with Your Pastors

> Obey your leaders and submit to them, for they are keeping watch over your souls, as those who will have to give an account. Let them do this with joy and not with groaning, for that would be of no advantage to you (Hebrews 13:17).

There comes a time when the Holy Spirit moves you to have a private conversation with someone in leadership at your church. Not for the purpose of rebelliously shaking your fist. But to sharpen and be sharpened. When humility is your pulse and sharpening is your goal, the outcome is always profitable.

> A church…will seldom take action to move toward something better unless it first realizes the need.[3]
>
> Wayne Cordeiro

Below are several keys to making the most out of conversations with your leaders.

Don't Look to Prove a Point

Trying to prove a point is pointless. When you enter your pastor's office, don't look to state your case about the areas your church is lacking. This is his church, his life's ministry. God placed him there for a reason. He's invested in it to a great degree.

Instead, bring up what you observed from evaluating your church and simply see how your pastor responds.

Ask Follow-Up Questions

Asking follow-up questions is essential. For years, I found myself dejected because I always took the pastor's first response and moved on even if the response didn't come close to answering my question. Now, instead of nodding and moving on, I ask another question. This has resulted in much deeper and worthwhile talks.

Write What You Want to Say

Not everyone enjoys writing, but we all benefit from writing down our thoughts. Doing so helps you narrow down exactly what you want to say and get a general idea of how you want to say it. When you have your letter written, it moves into your subconscious and is there for when you're actually talking with your pastor.

The other benefit of a letter is that you can also send it to your pastor as preparation for your meeting.

Be Humble

Be humble in everything. Instead of making definitive statements about the church, say, "Here's what I've been observing." Instead of coming across as though you know everything, say, "I don't fully know what I think about this—so I wanted to talk to you about it."

If you're not humble when you step into the pastor's office, leave. If you're not ready to listen 80 percent of the time and talk 20 percent of the time, leave. If you're not in it with a heart for God's glory, leave.

If you pass all these tests, use your 20 percent of talking time to examine the areas in which your church is lacking. Then let your pastor answer his 80 percent and leave it at that. One issue at a time, one meeting at a time.

Pray for Your Pastor

Not just for godly leadership of the flock, but also ask him personally, "How can I pray for you?" Then pray. Encourage him. Let him know that you'll be praying specifically about what he said.

The "Nevers"

- Never talk about the pastor behind his back, discussing his teaching.
- Never tell the pastor what he should support or promote.
- Never try to give him your convictions.
- Never try to be right. Try to be helpful in the growing of all believers in the church.

- Never challenge everything the pastor says. Don't make his ministry a horrible experience.

Writing a Letter to Your Pastor

- **Opening:** Thank the pastor for being your shepherd. Mention what you love about him most.

> Christian, are you ready for the day on which God will call you to account for how you have loved and served the church family, including your church leaders?[4]
>
> Mark Dever

- **Kernel of an Idea:** Let him know what's on your mind. Not the fully formed idea. Just the kernel of the reason you'd like to talk with him.

- **Outside Source:** A lot of the time, someone else has said what we want to say very clearly and concisely. Get on the Internet or grab an e-reader and see if this is the case for what you'd like to talk with your pastor about. Then copy and paste it into your email and add a sentence about why you included it. Bringing in an outside source really helps clarify your kernel of an idea.

- **Connect Your Outside Source to a Hypothetical Church Situation:** Now, get to your thoughts on how your kernel of an idea and outside source relate to your church. This is where you really get to the point—the areas in which your church may be lacking. Ask what your pastor thinks of your observations, and what, if anything, can be done to honor Jesus more. Discuss. Ask your pastor how he could see you and others as part of a solution.

- **Repeat Your Purpose:** Reaffirm why you approached him. Tell him again the purpose of your heart—to remain humble before God—and the burden of your heart—to explore with the pastor the questions and concerns stirring inside you.

Finally, if you write a letter, cut the pastor enormous slack. Say something like, "Please don't feel obligated to respond in length to this email. Maybe we can grab coffee sometime down the road and talk?"

The last thing you want to reaffirm is that you appreciate him and all that you learn from him. Then thank him for taking the time to hear you out, and sign off.

> Jesus is the only person who has the right to disown and give up on the church. But He never has. And He never will.[5]
>
> Joshua Harris

After You've Left

First, don't make a bigger deal out of your leaving than it needs to be. You don't need to announce all over social media that God has called you to leave, or your reasons for leaving. Look to stir up love and good works and unity, not anything else.

Second, don't force your convictions on someone else. Don't try to be other believers' Holy Spirit by asking them to join you in stepping away. Simply choose to speak love and truth into the lives of all believers.

Third, when God prompts you to leave your church, you enter a strange place that feels a lot like wilderness. You know you're in the right place at that moment, but you don't know which way you should walk. It's hazy. Look for a church, and don't stop. Pray for a church, and don't stop. Email and talk with people and meet with people about the churches around town, and don't stop. The wilderness is inevitable, and maybe even profitable for a time. But you eventually must find your way home, and your home is in the body of Christ.

Fourth, when looking for a new church, don't look for how the church can meet your needs. Instead, look for a place that loves God in spite of its faults. Look for a church where you can use your spiritual gifts. Remember, there's no such thing as a perfect church, so the main thing is to find an imperfect one that glorifies Jesus.

Fifth, if you're looking for good signs in a church, look for leaders who make themselves accountable to the church. Look for real humility, not false humility. Look for leaders willing to listen to honest questions and consider them in the context of Scripture. Look for a church that makes decisions out of faith, not fear. Look for a church that directs everyone to love God, love others, and make disciples. Look for a church caught up in love, grace, and forgiveness, not bitterness and hate.

Sixth, when you find a new church, don't be anonymous. Get to know people right away. Being disconnected from the body can be a very tempting time for believers. You want to get to know others who love Christ and who will encourage you and stir you to love and good deeds, just as you do the same to them.

> So the end of the matter is this: Live for God. Obey the Scriptures. Think of others before yourself. Be holy. Love Jesus. And as you do these things, do whatever else you like, with whomever you like, wherever you like, and you'll be walking in the will of God.[6]
>
> Kevin DeYoung

Seventh, while there's not a ton of time to be investing in an old church family and a new church family, you can at least keep in touch with those in your old church. Share a coffee now and then. Have dinner. Don't buy into the idea that you're completely separated because you go to different churches, or because you have differing views about God. See each other as brothers and sisters who will spend eternity in heaven together.

What Now?

Watch this chapter's video at www.calledtostay.com.

Get the download of the "When To Leave and What to Consider" here: www.calledtostay.com/downloads.

"Here's what I'm considering about my church today:"— Add what you'd like to say, post this as your Facebook status, and I'll join the conversation (just remember to tag me).

What's Next

It's time we, in full force, usher in the age of the Infiltrator.

CHAPTER 10

Staying

"If it were possible, God, we'd jump into these pouches," my pastor prayed just before the ushers passed around the offering bags.

That picture has stuck with me.

> Satan has a simple mission: to keep lost people lost. Among his numerous strategies, one of his favorites is to keep Christians convinced that ministry must be left to professionals.[1]
>
> Ed Stetzer

But after writing this book, it's hard for me to sit through an offering without smiling. Because I no longer picture my brothers and sisters just diving into the pouches.

I picture them ripping through the bottoms and hitting the church's floor.

Because one of the greatest commitments we could ever make to Christ is to stay in his church and infiltrate.

The Progressive Way to Be Like Jesus

The top five reasons people leave the church can be boiled down to one: They do not infiltrate. At least, that's one way to interpret this research: [2]

- Twenty-eight percent of people leave because the church is not helping them develop spiritually. Infiltrators prompt spiritual development in both themselves and in others by examining their walk with Jesus, engaging the power of the Holy Spirit, and embracing the childlikeness Christ says we need.

- Twenty percent leave because they don't feel engaged in

meaningful church work. Infiltrators never stop doing meaningful church work because they're always pointing others toward greater commitment to Jesus.

- Eighteen percent leave because other church members are judgmental. Infiltrators set a new tone of unity to counteract the misguided judgment of others.

- Sixteen percent leave because their pastor isn't any good. Infiltrators challenge their pastors to more spiritual depth by engaging with them in all love, humility, and boldness.

- Sixteen percent leave because there are too many changes happening. Infiltrators disregard the numerous changes while focusing on the main change needed: heart change.

Many believe that abandoning the church is the progressive way to move toward Jesus. But from everything I see in Scripture, the progressive way to move toward Jesus is to be like him in your church.

And a great way to be like Jesus in your church is to infiltrate.

We Cannot Love Without Hurt

When I look at the exodus from the church, I don't see a movement that mirrors Jesus. I see a movement of purging and disunity, bitterness and grudges.

> Nothing can be more cruel than the tenderness that consigns another to his sin. Nothing can be more compassionate than the severe rebuke that calls a brother back from the path of sin.[3]
>
> Dietrich Bonhoeffer

This isn't the way of Christ.

To truly love someone is to resign yourself to hurt. We cannot love someone without adding hurt to our lives. Because true love, unconditional love, is established through hurt. Hurt proves that love is true.

Jesus suffered horrifically on the cross for us. He was betrayed by one of his closest followers. He was called a liar and a sinner. He was spat upon, whipped, and tortured. He was abandoned by his dearest friends. He took nails into his hands and feet and a spear into his side. He died at the hands of his people, for his people.

By this we know his love is true.

> Live together in the forgiveness of your sins, for without it no human fellowship, least of all a marriage, can survive. Don't insist on your rights, don't blame each other, don't judge or condemn each other, don't find fault with each other, but accept each other as you are, and forgive each other every day from the bottom of your hearts.[4]
>
> Dietrich Bonhoeffer

When we invest our lives in the body of Christ, we will be hurt as well. But this is how we prove our love for Jesus is true—by hurting for who he hurt for and by giving our lives to those for whom he gave his life.

Being hurt by the church doesn't give us the right to leave her. It gives us the opportunity to love her anyway, just as Jesus loves us anyway.

Lashing out at the church won't heal your hurt. Only Christ can. Don't go out of your way to find the church's biggest warts and broadcast them live for the world to see. That doesn't do anyone any good. It simply feeds your hurt and keeps it fully alive.

Refuse to be the one spoken of in Proverbs 18:1-2, who separated himself and became interested in his own opinions of God and the Word. Refuse to surround yourself only with Christians who live and think as you live and think.

Refuse the desire to be a churchless Christian.

Let this be the age of the Infiltrator. The age of grace and forgiveness. The age of love for God and others. Don't lose one precious day. Choose to infiltrate and watch as others emerge to join you in the cause.

From the least of these to the greatest, from the stained glass to the strobe lights, we are the church—and we were created to do life together in the body of Christ.

> By this we know love, that he laid down his life for us, and we ought to lay down our lives for the brothers (1 John 3:16).

A NOTE FROM THE AUTHOR

I don't know everything about Jesus and his church. Not even close. This book is merely my best attempt to help others who are facing the same struggles I've faced and am still facing. I would love to continue the dialogue with you about what's working for you, what isn't, and how you and I can continue making the bride of Christ more beautiful for Jesus. Please stop by, join the discussion, and leave your questions and comments at https://www.facebook.com/CalebJenningsBreakey.

1. **What prompted you to write this book?**

   Called to Stay has kind of been a living journal. God didn't stir me to write about the church. Instead, he nudged me to stay in a church I'd grown bitter toward. It was only after the tears, stomach churns, and wounded pride that I could look over my shoulder and say: "I get it now. Thank you, Jesus. Let's do this. Let's write it down."

2. **From your experience, what is the most common reason Millennials give for leaving the church? Does this reason have any validity?**

   Many leave because the way of the world just seems better. But some leave because the time they spend in church seems ineffective in a broken world that Jesus is calling us to redeem. This second reason has validity, but most people use it as an excuse while ignoring God's commands about (1) meeting together in a way that doesn't exclude the messy and immature; (2) structure and leadership; and (3) Christ's great mandate to forgive our debtors and to sacrificially love one another.

3. **Can Christians follow Jesus and still leave the church? Is it possible to be a disciple of Christ and be disconnected from His Body?**

   God gives us all kinds of assignments. And while we are *never* commanded to stop meeting together, discipling each other, or extending sacrificial love to one another, we *can* be given assignments that remove us from Christian fellowship. If you are one of these believers, the most important thing is to discern whether you're hearing from the Holy Spirit—or simply hearing what you want to hear.

4. **Some statistics suggest that Millennials are *not* leaving the church in the numbers often suggested. Youth have always left the church and tend to return as they have families and get older. Is it possible the numbers are being skewed by one group or another to serve their purposes? On what grounds do you think Millennial defection is a legitimate issue that churches must face?**

I think many numbers are skewed. That's why I mostly avoided the use of statistics in *Called to Stay*. I wanted to invest more in what Scripture says about staying in messy gatherings of believers than how many are leaving or returning.

Should churches be concerned over the juicy headlines about declining church attendance? Sort of. I think churches should mostly concern themselves with making disciples who speak the truth in love to one another, embrace God's plan for structure and leadership, and long to build Christ's church through *their* church.

5. **Your book is intended to bridge the divide between the church and Millennial "leavers." As a Millennial yourself, where do you think the healing starts? What percentage of blame falls on the church and on Millennials, and who should make the first move to bridge the divide?**

One hundred percent of the blame falls on the church, and the other one hundred percent falls on the Millennials. The fact is that blame is sin—and no matter who's got more of it on our faces, we all need a shower of grace. We are all responsible for loving the sin-slingers and forgiving them. *Daily.*

As for who must bridge the divide, that person is you. We're in this together, and we must never, ever belittle the enormous influence each of us has. A spark blown upon by God's Holy Spirit is a spark that *burns*.

6. **You raised $10,000 through Kickstarter to fund a DVD project for this book. That must have been incredibly encouraging. Tell me about the initial responses you're getting to the book.**

The response has blown me away. Men and women of God are rallying. They're making sacrifices. They're going out on limbs. They're saying things and doing things that they haven't said or done before. The body is *moving*—and it's an awesome sight.

Interview by Mike Duran

Now that you've finished *Called to Stay*, why not let the world know? Share these tweets with your followers!

For every church in which Jesus would turn tables, there are 100 more in which he would say, "Overcome." **#Staying**

It's time to radiate the presence of Jesus not only to the lost, but also to the body of Christ. **#Staying**

Leaving a sick person is easy. Healing her is hard. Which sounds more like Jesus? **#Staying**

Start rattling souls in your church. **#Staying**

Build the Church through YOUR church. **#Staying**

Loving the Church is hard, but Jesus won't leave her. Neither should we. **#Staying**

If we're not moving toward love, unity, and a deep hunger for Jesus in our churches, then we're the problem. **#Staying**

Rare is the believer who looks within his or her church and thinks, "Who do you want me to invest in, God?" **#Staying**

Get to know your fellow messy believers in the body of Christ. Don't judge them or leave them. **#Staying**

If our ultimate goal is to be like Jesus, then forgiving the unforgivable in our churches is the biggest step. **#Staying**

Pour the energy it takes to criticize the Church into loving the unlovely within her. **#Staying**

Need an answer to your messed-up church? The answer is you. #Staying

Those who leave the church in order to be the church end up needing a church. #Staying

God's given us the responsibility to love the messy church, forgive her, and give our lives to her. #Staying

Help move the shallow to authentic, the heady to the heart, and the fearful to true faith. #Staying

Help others in the church live out the uncomplicated gospel of loving God and others. #Staying

Help others in your church see that the body is a mission, a movement, a calling. #Staying

Don't try to change people, but let God use you in the growth of others. #Staying

How might you challenge a shortcoming in your church in a gentle, loving, and encouraging way? #Staying

Following Jesus and staying in church are not at odds. They go hand-in-hand. #Staying

Help bring people back to truth. Back to commitment. Back to conviction. #Staying

It doesn't matter if the Church is sick. It matters what you do to make her healthier or sicker. #Staying

The way to move toward Jesus is to be like him in your church. #Staying

To truly love someone is to resign yourself to hurt. This includes the Bride of Christ. #Staying

Being hurt by the Church doesn't give us the right to leave her. It gives us the opportunity to love her anyway. #Staying

https://twitter.com/CalebBreakey

NOTES

Chapter 1: Save the Girl

1. David Powlison, "Can I Grow in Holiness Without the Local Church?," *Desiring God* (blog), August 24, 2012, http://www.desiringgod.org/blog/posts/can-i-grow-in-holiness-without-the -local-church.

2. Stephen Mansfield, *Healing Your Church Hurt: What to Do When You Still Love God but Have Been Wounded by His People* (Carol Stream, IL: Tyndale House Publishers, 2012), 2.

3. Ed Stetzer and Thom S. Rainer, *Transformational Church: Creating a New Scorecard for Congregations* (Nashville, TN: B&H Publishing Group, 2010), 8.

4. Ibid., 94.

5. Dietrich Bonhoeffer, *Life Together: The Classic Exploration of Christian Community* (New York: Harper & Row Publishers, 1954), 89.

6. Joshua Harris, *Stop Dating the Church: Fall in Love with the Family of God* (Colorado Springs, CO: Multnomah Publishers, 2004), 31.

7. Ed Stetzer, *Subversive: Living as Agents of Gospel Transformation* (Nashville, TN: B&H Publishing Group, 2012), 100.

8. Mark Dever, *What Is a Healthy Church?* (Wheaton, IL: Crossway, 2007), 16.

9. Mark Dever, *Twelve Challenges Churches Face* (Wheaton, IL: Crossway, 2008), 153.

Chapter 2: Why You Must Stay

1. Stephen Mansfield, *Healing Your Church Hurt: What to Do When You Still Love God but Have Been Wounded by His People* (Carol Stream, IL: Tyndale House Publishers, 2012), 15-16.

2. Ed Stetzer and Thom S. Rainer, *Transformational Church: Creating a New Scorecard for Congregations* (Nashville, TN: B&H Publishing Group, 2010), 133.

3. Ibid., 3.

4. Ed Stetzer, *Subversive: Living as Agents of Gospel Transformation* (Nashville, TN: B&H Publishing Group, 2012), 54.

5. Ibid., 53.

6. Joshua Harris, *Stop Dating the Church: Fall in Love with the Family of God* (Colorado Springs, CO: Multnomah Publishers, 2004), 58.

7. Dietrich Bonhoeffer, *Life Together: The Classic Exploration of Christian Community* (New York: Harper & Row Publishers, 1954), 27.

8. Mark Dever, *What Is a Healthy Church?* (Wheaton, IL: Crossway, 2007), 36.

9. Stetzer and Rainer, *Transformational Church*, 116.

10. Thabiti M. Anyabwile, *What Is a Healthy Church Member?* (Wheaton, IL: Crossway, 2008), 66.

11. Mark Dever, *Twelve Challenges Churches Face* (Wheaton, IL: Crossway, 2008), 12.

12. Bonhoeffer, *Life Together*, 38.

Chapter 3: Infiltrating Q & A

1. Wayne Cordeiro, *The Irresistible Church: 12 Traits of a Church Heaven Applauds* (Bloomington, MN: Bethany House Publishers, 2011), 15.

2. Ibid., 16.

Chapter 4: Where to Start

1. Dietrich Bonhoeffer, *Life Together: The Classic Exploration of Christian Community* (New York: Harper & Row Publishers, 1954), 96.

2. Wayne Cordeiro, *The Irresistible Church: 12 Traits of a Church Heaven Applauds* (Bloomington, MN: Bethany House Publishers, 2011), 134.

3. Ibid., 49.

4. Ed Stetzer and Thom S. Rainer, *Transformational Church: Creating a New Scorecard for Congregations* (Nashville, TN: B&H Publishing Group, 2010), 56.

5. Joshua Harris, *Stop Dating the Church: Fall in Love with the Family of God* (Colorado Springs, CO: Multnomah Publishers, 2004), 95.

6. Cordeiro, *The Irresistible Church*, 17.

7. Stetzer and Rainer, *Transformational Church*, 230.

8. Cordeiro, *The Irresistible Church*, 143.

9. Mark Dever, *Twelve Challenges Churches Face* (Wheaton, IL: Crossway, 2008), 42.

10. Peter Scazzero, *The Emotionally Healthy Church: A Strategy for Discipleship that Actually Changes Lives* (Grand Rapids, MI: Zondervan, 2010), 81.

Chapter 5: Who You Must Embrace

1. Francis Chan, *Forgotten God: Reversing Our Tragic Neglect of the Holy Spirit* (Colorado Springs, CO: David C. Cook, 2009), 54.

2. Bruce Wilkinson and David Kopp, *You Were Born for This: 7 Keys to a Life of Predictable Miracles* (Colorado Springs, CO: Multnomah Books, 2009), 19.

3. Chan, *Forgotten God*, 142.

4. Wayne Cordeiro, *The Irresistible Church: 12 Traits of a Church Heaven Applauds* (Bloomington, MN: Bethany House Publishers, 2011), 22.

5. Wilkinson and Kopp, *You Were Born for This*, 21.

6. Chan, *Forgotten God*, 132.

7. Ibid., 88.

8. Wilkinson and Kopp, *You Were Born for This*, 34.

9. Cordeiro, *The Irresistible Church*, 120.

10. Chan, *Forgotten God*, 69.

11. Ibid., 87.

12. Ibid., 85.

13. Ed Stetzer, *Subversive: Living as Agents of Gospel Transformation* (Nashville, TN: B&H Publishing Group, 2012), 202.

Chapter 6: What Comes Next

1. Peter Scazzero, *The Emotionally Healthy Church: A Strategy for Discipleship that Actually Changes Lives* (Grand Rapids, MI: Zondervan, 2010), 4.

2. James MacDonald, *Vertical Church: What Every Heart Longs For. What Every Church Can Be* (Colorado Springs, CO: David C. Cook, 2012), 169.

3. Francis Chan, *Forgotten God: Reversing Our Tragic Neglect of the Holy Spirit* (Colorado Springs, CO: David C. Cook, 2009), 162.

4. Dietrich Bonhoeffer, *Life Together: The Classic Exploration of Christian Community* (New York: Harper & Row Publishers, 1954), 101.

5. Wayne Cordeiro, *The Irresistible Church: 12 Traits of a Church Heaven Applauds* (Bloomington, MN: Bethany House Publishers, 2011), 118.

6. MacDonald, *Vertical Church*, 179.

7. Cordeiro, *The Irresistible Church*, 73.

8. Stephen Mansfield, *Healing Your Church Hurt: What to Do When You Still Love God but Have Been Wounded by His People* (Carol Stream, IL: Tyndale House Publishers, 2012), 154.

9. Ed Stetzer, *Subversive: Living as Agents of Gospel Transformation* (Nashville, TN: B&H Publishing Group, 2012), 74.

Chapter 7: How to Infiltrate—One

1. Timothy George and John Woodbridge, *The Mark of Jesus: Loving in a Way the World Can See* (Chicago, IL: Moody Publishers, 2005), 92.

2. Stephen Mansfield, *Healing Your Church Hurt: What to Do When You Still Love God but Have Been Wounded by His People* (Carol Stream, IL: Tyndale House Publishers, 2012), 30.

3. Ed Stetzer, *Subversive: Living as Agents of Gospel Transformation* (Nashville, TN: B&H Publishing Group, 2012), 117.

4. Dietrich Bonhoeffer, *Life Together: The Classic Exploration of Christian Community* (New York: Harper & Row Publishers, 1954), 34.

5. Ed Stetzer and Thom S. Rainer, *Transformational Church: Creating a New Scorecard for Congregations* (Nashville, TN: B&H Publishing Group, 2010), 48-49.

6. Wayne Cordeiro, *The Irresistible Church: 12 Traits of a Church Heaven Applauds* (Bloomington, MN: Bethany House Publishers, 2011), 103.

7. Joshua Harris, *Stop Dating the Church: Fall in Love with the Family of God* (Colorado Springs, CO: Multnomah Publishers, 2004), 59.

8. Stetzer and Rainer, *Transformational Church*, 181.

9. Stephen W. Smith, *The Jesus Life: Eight Ways to Recover Authentic Christianity* (Colorado Springs, CO: David C. Cook, 2012), 189.

10. Ibid., 144.

11. Stetzer and Rainer, *Transformational Church*, 189.

12. Stetzer, *Subversive*, 128.

Chapter 8: How to Infiltrate—Two

1. Ed Stetzer and Thom S. Rainer, *Transformational Church: Creating a New Scorecard for Congregations* (Nashville, TN: B&H Publishing Group, 2010), 115.

2. Mark Dever, *What Is a Healthy Church?* (Wheaton, IL: Crossway, 2007), 35.

3. Dietrich Bonhoeffer, *Life Together: The Classic Exploration of Christian Community* (New York: Harper & Row Publishers, 1954), 23.

4. Wayne Cordeiro, *The Irresistible Church: 12 Traits of a Church Heaven Applauds* (Bloomington, MN: Bethany House Publishers, 2011), 96.

5. Mark Dever, *Twelve Challenges Churches Face* (Wheaton, IL: Crossway, 2008), 181.

6. Stephen Mansfield, *Healing Your Church Hurt: What to Do When You Still Love God but Have Been Wounded by His People* (Carol Stream, IL: Tyndale House Publishers, 2012), 31.

7. Ed Stetzer, *Subversive: Living as Agents of Gospel Transformation* (Nashville, TN: B&H Publishing Group, 2012), 21-22.

8. Joshua Harris, *Stop Dating the Church: Fall in Love with the Family of God* (Colorado Springs, CO: Multnomah Publishers, 2004), 61.

9. Stetzer, *Subversive*, 70.

10. Cordeiro, *The Irresistible Church*, 37.

11. Peter Scazzero, *The Emotionally Healthy Church: A Strategy for Discipleship that Actually Changes Lives* (Grand Rapids, MI: Zondervan, 2010), 218.

12. Stetzer and Rainer, *Transformational Church*, 177.

13. Thabiti M. Anyabwile, *What Is a Healthy Church Member?* (Wheaton, IL: Crossway, 2008), 36.

14. Scazzero, *The Emotionally Healthy Church*, 5.

15. Bonhoeffer, *Life Together*, 24.

16. Stetzer, *Subversive*, 184.

17. Bonhoeffer, *Life Together*, 35.

18. Stephen W. Smith, *The Jesus Life: Eight Ways to Recover Authentic Christianity* (Colorado Springs, CO: David C. Cook, 2012), 206.

19. Bonhoeffer, *Life Together*, 97.

20. Scazzero, *The Emotionally Healthy Church*, 189.

21. Smith, *The Jesus Life*, 122.

22. Stetzer and Rainer, *Transformational Church*, 83.

23. Bonhoeffer, *Life Together*, 104.

24. Dever, *What Is a Healthy Church?*, 29.

25. Mansfield, *Healing Your Church Hurt*, 50.

26. Anyabwile, *What Is a Healthy Church Member?*, 58.

Chapter 9: When to Leave

1. Thabiti M. Anyabwile, *What Is a Healthy Church Member?* (Wheaton, IL: Crossway, 2008), 102.

2. Joshua Harris, *Stop Dating the Church: Fall in Love with the Family of God* (Colorado Springs, CO: Multnomah Publishers, 2004), 97.

3. Wayne Cordeiro, *The Irresistible Church: 12 Traits of a Church Heaven Applauds* (Bloomington, MN: Bethany House Publishers, 2011), 28.

4. Mark Dever, *What Is a Healthy Church?* (Wheaton, IL: Crossway, 2007), 31.

5. Harris, *Stop Dating the Church*, 40.

6. Kevin DeYoung, *Just Do Something: A Liberating Approach to Finding God's Will* (Chicago, IL: Moody Publishers, 2009), 122.

Chapter 10: Staying

1. Ed Stetzer and Thom S. Rainer, *Transformational Church: Creating a New Scorecard for Congregations* (Nashville, TN: B&H Publishing Group, 2010), 94.

2. "LifeWay Research Finds Reason Adults Switch Churches," LifeWay Christian Resources, accessed March 7, 2013, http://www.lifeway.com/Article LifeWay-Research-finds-reason-adults-switch-churches.

3. Dietrich Bonhoeffer, *Life Together: The Classic Exploration of Christian Community* (New York: Harper & Row Publishers, 1954), 107.

4. Dietrich Bonhoeffer, *Letters and Papers from Prison*, ed. Eberhard Bethge (New York: Macmillan, 1972), 46.

Caleb Jennings Breakey is a former journalist and the author of *Called to Stay*. His speculative novel, *Unleashed*, won first place in the 2012 ACFW Genesis Contest. Caleb is a frequent conference speaker who loves leading others in discussions about relationships, the church, and radically following Jesus. He lives in Washington state with his beautiful wife and writing companion, Brittney.

Connect with Caleb at
facebook.com/CalebJenningsBreakey